D1321665

Pearson Edexcel GCSE (9–1)

History

Superpower relations and the Cold War, 1941–91

Revision Guide & Workbook + App

Series Consultant: Harry Smith

Author: Brian Dowse

A note from the publisher

In order to ensure that this resource offers high-quality support for the associated Pearson qualification, it has been through a review process by the awarding body. This process confirms that this resource fully covers the teaching and learning content of the specification or part of a specification at which it is aimed. It also confirms that it demonstrates an appropriate balance between the development of subject skills, knowledge and understanding, in addition to preparation for assessment.

Endorsement does not cover any guidance on assessment activities or processes (e.g. practise questions or advice on how to answer assessment questions), included in the resource nor does it prescribe any particular approach to the teaching or delivery of a related course.

While the publishers have made every attempt to ensure that advice on the qualification and its assessment is accurate, the official specification and associated assessment guidance materials are the only authoritative source of information and should always be referred to for definitive guidance.

Pearson examiners have not contributed to any sections in this resource relevant to examination papers for which they have responsibility.

Examiners will not use endorsed resources as a source of material for any assessment set by Pearson.

Endorsement of a resource does not mean that the resource is required to achieve this Pearson qualification, nor does it mean that it is the only suitable material available to support the qualification, and any resource lists produced by the awarding body shall include this and other appropriate resources.

For the full range of Pearson revision titles across KS2, 11+, KS3, GCSE, Functional Skills, AS/A Level and BTEC visit:
www.pearsonschools.co.uk/revise

Contents

. . . .

A small bit of small print

Pearson Edexcel publishes Sample Assessment Material and the Specification on its website. This is the official content and this book should be used in conjunction with it. The questions in *Now try this* have been written to help you practise every topic in the book. Remember: the real exam questions may not look like this.

The beginning of the Cold War

Before the Cold War Britain, the USA and the Soviet Union worked together as members of the Grand Alliance, which was created in 1941 to defeat Nazi Germany. The leaders of these countries met three times: at Tehran (1943), Yalta (1945) and Potsdam (1945).

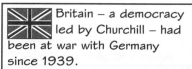 Britain – a democracy led by Churchill – had been at war with Germany since 1939.

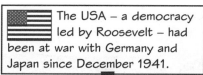 The USA – a democracy led by Roosevelt – had been at war with Germany and Japan since December 1941.

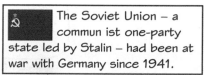 The Soviet Union – a commun ist one-party state led by Stalin – had been at war with Germany since 1941.

The Grand Alliance therefore was a 'marriage of convenience', in which three countries shared the aim of defeating their common enemy – Nazi Germany.

The Tehran Conference (November–December 1943)

- ✓ The USA and Britain agreed to open up a second front by invading Nazi-occupied Europe.
- ✓ The Soviet Union would declare war on Japan once Germany was defeated.
- ✓ The boundaries of Poland would be moved westwards; Poland would gain territory from Germany and lose it to the Soviet Union.
- ✓ It was also agreed that an international body would be set up to settle future disputes between countries. This set the scene for the establishment of the United Nations.

The Yalta Conference (February 1945)

- ✓ Germany, when defeated, would be reduced in size, divided and demilitarised. It would have to pay reparations.
- ✓ Europe would be rebuilt along the lines of the Atlantic Charter. Countries would have democratic elections.
- ✓ The UN (United Nations) would be set up.
- ✓ The Soviet Union would declare war on Japan once Germany was defeated.
- ✓ Poland would be in the 'Soviet sphere of influence' but run on a broader democratic basis.

The Potsdam Conference (July–August 1945)

- ✓ A Council of Foreign Ministers was set up to organise the rebuilding of Europe.
- ✓ The Nazi Party was banned and war criminals were to be prosecuted.
- ✓ Germany was to be reduced in size and divided into four zones of occupation run by Britain, France, the USA and the Soviet Union.
- ✓ Berlin was also to be divided up into zones of occupation.
- ✓ The Soviet Union was to receive 25% of the output from the other three occupied zones.

The outcomes of the conferences

Remember: while Britain, the USA and the Soviet Union were able to work together to defeat Germany, who had surrendered in May 1945, tension was increasing between the wartime allies. Differences were beginning to emerge over the future of Germany and Eastern Europe. Moreover, Roosevelt's death had led to Truman becoming president and he was much more distrustful of the Soviet Union.

Students often confuse what happened at these conferences. Make sure you know the differences and the similarities between them.

Now try this

1 Explain what was agreed at the Tehran, Yalta and Potsdam Conferences.
2 Draw up a timeline of the key events involving the Grand Alliance between November 1943 and July 1945.

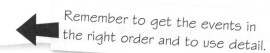 Remember to get the events in the right order and to use detail.

The end of the Grand Alliance

Truman, Stalin and Churchill were the leaders of the USA, the Soviet Union and Britain when the war against Germany ended in 1945.

> Europe should be democratic – a capitalist democracy. Roosevelt believed that democracy meant different political parties working to win voters' support in free elections.

> Churchill, Roosevelt and Stalin meeting in Yalta in 1945.

> What should happen to Germany? Germany should have to pay reparations, ensuring that it is never strong enough to start another war.

> What should happen to Germany? Germany should be rebuilt.

> Europe should be democratic – a communist democracy. Stalin believed that because only communism truly represented the workers, democracies could only be communist.

> The USA was the first to build an atomic bomb, which gave it an unbeatable advantage (until 1949, when the Soviet Union caught up).

> The Soviet Union didn't do what it said it would do in Poland: the government was supposed to include multiple political parties, but actually was only a communist democracy.

After Germany surrendered in May 1945, the Grand Alliance started to come to an end. Roosevelt was the key figure in holding the Alliance together. He believed that the United States could work with the Soviet Union after the war came to an end through the United Nations. His successor, Truman, was, like Churchill, more suspicious of the Soviet Union and this increased tension between the Allies.

The end of the Grand Alliance

The USA dropped atomic bombs on Japan in August 1945. This gave them a huge military advantage over other countries.

Roosevelt was prepared to work with Stalin but he died in April 1945 and was replaced by Truman.
Truman trusted Stalin much less, as he had broken the promises he made over Poland at Yalta. He felt that, thanks to the atomic bomb, he could push Stalin around at the Potsdam Conference.

Stalin disliked the way in which Truman had tried to push him around at Potsdam in 1945.

Increased tension between the superpowers and the start of the cold war.

Britain had finished on the winning side in 1945 but was economically exhausted by the war. It was therefore unable to stand up to the Soviet Union on its own and became only an ally of the United States. The Cold War therefore became increasingly about the relationship between the two superpowers, the United States and the Soviet Union.

Now try this

1 Explain how Roosevelt's death increased tension between the USA and the Soviet Union.
2 The Soviet Union said communism could be democratic, too. What was the Western criticism of communist democracy?

The breakdown of trust

Without a common enemy to fight, tensions between the USA and the Soviet Union intensified. Neither side trusted the other due to ideological differences and the fact that the USA, unlike the Soviet Union, possessed nuclear weapons.

Ideology

Understanding ideology – a set of political ideas about how society should be run – is key to understanding the Cold War. The USA and the Soviet Union had opposing ideologies.

The USA, Britain and other capitalist countries

Said communism enslaved people to the state. Capitalism was based on freedom and democracy:

- Everyone should be free to make money for themselves.

- Individuals are better at deciding what to make/sell than the state.

- Trade between countries makes everyone richer.

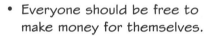

The Soviet Union and other communist countries

Said capitalism exploited the workers to make the rich even richer. Communism was based on fairness:

- Capitalism only makes some people rich by exploiting everyone else.

- Individuals are not as strong as everyone working together for the same aim.

- The state should take control of the economy and run it to benefit everyone.

The Long Telegram (1946)

A secret report from the US ambassador Kennan in Moscow to President Truman said:

- the Soviet Union saw capitalism as a threat to communism that had to be destroyed

- the Soviet Union was building its military power

- peace between a communist Soviet Union and a capitalist USA was not possible.

Novikov's Telegram (1946)

A report from Novikov, Soviet ambassador to the USA, told Stalin that:

- the USA wanted world domination and was building up its military strength

- the Soviet Union was the only country left after the war that could stand up to the USA

- the USA was preparing its people for war with the Soviet Union.

Ideological differences and the atomic bomb had made relations between the superpowers worse. The USA saw the Soviet Union as a threat to its economic interests in Europe. The Soviet Union feared and resented the USA's nuclear monopoly, which did not end until 1949.

Now try this

Creating lists like this will enable you to understand key terms and topics and draw conclusions about them.

1 Create a table with two columns, one for capitalism and the other for communism. Then, insert any words that relate to either, matching words by their opposing term (e.g. capitalism: individual / communism: collective).

2 Now answer the following questions in the light of the table you have just created:
   (a) What was communism's main criticism of capitalism?
   (b) What was capitalism's main criticism of communism?

3 Why did trust between the USA and the Soviet Union decrease between 1945 and 1947?

Satellite states

Between 1947 and 1949, the Soviet Union spread its sphere of influence to neighbouring countries. Countries like Poland and Hungary became 'satellite states' under the control of the Soviet Union.

Communism and 'free' elections

- At the Yalta and Potsdam conferences, the Soviet Union agreed to free elections in the countries in its sphere of influence.

- However, elections were fixed to make sure the Communist Party won and non-communists were removed from government.

- Once in control, the communists shut down the opposition parties and each country became a single-party state.

Fixing elections and then shutting down opposition parties was known as 'salami tactics'.

Land taken by Soviet Union at the end of the Second World War
Soviet-controlled communist countries
Non Soviet-controlled communist countries

Soviet expansion in Europe, 1945–48.

The growing Soviet influence in Eastern Europe

Country	How it became communist
Bulgaria	A communist government was elected in 1945, and all elected non-communists were executed.
Romania	A communist-led coalition took power. However, by 1947 the communists had taken over and Romania became a one-party state.
Poland	At Yalta Stalin promised to set up a joint communist/non-communist government. He then invited 16 non-communist leaders to Moscow and arrested them. Thousands of non-communists were arrested. The communists then 'won' the 1947 election.
Hungary	The communists lost the 1945 election but the communist leader Rakosi took control of the secret police, executed and imprisoned his opponents and turned Hungary into a communist state.
Czechoslovakia	Edward Benes set up a coalition government. However, the communists retained control of the army, the radio and the secret police. In 1948 they seized power completely, turning the country into a communist state.
East Germany	The original Soviet zone of occupation in Germany, it became a communist state in October 1949.

The impact of the Soviet occupation of Eastern Europe on superpower relations

- The USA saw the Soviet takeover of Eastern Europe as a betrayal of the Yalta agreement, in which Stalin had made promises about holding democratic elections.

- Others saw it as evidence of Soviet expansion: Eastern Europe was a stepping-stone to a Soviet takeover of Western Europe.

- The USA was determined to contain communism through military and economic assistance: the Truman Doctrine and Marshall Aid.

- The Soviet Union argued it needed to control Eastern Europe as a buffer zone, protecting it from attack by the West. The US response was unnecessary and unreasonable.

Now try this

Describe how Stalin was able to gain control of Eastern Europe between 1945 and 1950.

The Truman Doctrine and the Marshall Plan

In response to the spread of Soviet control in Eastern Europe, the USA stepped up its involvement in Europe, and the Soviet Union was determined to defend itself against any threats from the West. The USA was determined to stop the spread of communism, and the Soviet Union was determined to defend itself against Western attack. Europe was the centre of this ideological 'battleground'. The Truman Doctrine and the Marshall Plan thus increased tension between the United States and the Soviet Union.

Truman's concerns

- Europe was devastated after the war.
- In many countries people had no money, no jobs and were feeling hopeless.
- Communism was attractive to these people, especially in France and Italy: it made sure everyone had enough.
- Many in Eastern Europe had been liberated from Nazi rule by the Soviets.
- Countries like Poland, Romania and Bulgaria had already had communist governments forced on them and Truman feared this could happen in other countries too.
- Some governments (e.g. Greece and Turkey) were too poor to combat communist revolutions in their own countries.
- If Greece and Turkey became communist, then other countries across Europe and the Middle East would follow. This was known as the Domino Theory.

Post-war Berlin. Much of Europe had been destroyed during the war. Many people were homeless and starving. Truman feared that this could lead to people electing communist governments.

The Truman Doctrine (1947)

In a speech in 1947, US President Truman set out why the USA should get involved:

- ✓ Countries faced a choice between either capitalism or communism.
- ✓ Communism was bad because it meant people could not be free.
- ✓ The USA must try to contain (hold back) this spread of communism.
- ✓ The USA should provide money and troops (if necessary) to help free governments to combat communist takeovers.

The Truman Doctrine was all about stopping the spread of communism. The USA was prepared to use both military and economic methods to prevent this from happening.

The Marshall Plan (1947)

- ✓ About $13 billion from USA to help rebuild Europe.
- ✓ Communism appealed most to people with nothing to lose, so the Marshall Plan hoped to stop communism by giving people a stake in the capitalist system.
- ✓ Countries must trade with the USA to get the money.
- ✓ Sixteen Western European countries took the money including Britain, France and West Germany.
- ✓ The Soviet Union criticised the Marshall Plan as an attack on them because it threatened communist control in Eastern Europe.

Now try this

1 Explain **two** consequences of the Truman Doctrine and the Marshall Plan.
2 Explain why the USA hoped that the Marshall Plan would combat the spread of communism.

Cominform, Comecon and NATO

The establishment of NATO in Western Europe matched the setting up of Cominform and Comecon in Eastern Europe.

Cominform

Cominform stood for the Communist Information Bureau. Stalin set it up in 1947. The bureau organised all the communist parties in Europe and arranged their leadership so they would do what Moscow told them to.

Key points:

- ✓ Cominform got rid of any opposition to the Soviet Union's control in satellite states.
- ✓ It encouraged communist parties in Western countries to block Marshall Plan assistance.

Comecon

Comecon stood for the Council for Mutual Economic Assistance. Stalin set it up in 1949. It was the Soviet Union's alternative to the Marshall Plan.

Key points:

- ✓ It built up trade links between Comecon countries.
- ✓ It also prevented Comecon countries signing up to the Marshall Plan.
- ✓ Comecon included the Soviet Union, Bulgaria, Czechoslovakia, Hungary, Poland, Romania, Albania and, from 1950, the German Democratic Republic (East Germany).

Consequences

Western Europe was now in one camp. It was linked to the USA through the Marshall Plan and the US policy of containment of communism.

Eastern Europe was now in one camp. It was tied to the Soviet Union as satellite states and the Soviet Union believed socialist revolution would spread worldwide.

Europe was now divided into two spheres of influence: Western Europe (capitalist and pro-American) and Eastern Europe (communist and controlled by the Soviet Union). The line that divided these two spheres of influence was known as the Iron Curtain.

The North Atlantic Treaty Organisation (NATO)

- ✓ NATO was set up in 1949. It was a military alliance made up of the United States, Britain, Canada, Holland, Belgium, France, Denmark and Norway. West Germany joined in 1955.
- ✓ NATO was a military alliance based around the principle of collective security; if one country was attacked other countries had to assist it.
- ✓ NATO was directed against a possible military attack from the Soviet Union on Western Europe.

The significance of NATO

- ✓ NATO showed that, after the Berlin Blockade and the Soviet Union's own development of the atomic bomb, neither the United States nor Western European governments were prepared to accept future Soviet aggression.
- ✓ The Soviet Union therefore turned to strengthening its control over Eastern Europe, resulting in the formation of the Warsaw Pact in 1955.
- ✓ There were now two military alliances, NATO and the Warsaw Pact, facing each other across the Iron Curtain.

Now try this

Why was Stalin so keen to prevent satellite countries getting money from the Marshall Plan?

Germany and the Cold War

The Allies were unable to agree about Germany's future. A short-term solution, agreed at Potsdam in July 1945, was to divide the country and its capital, Berlin, into zones of military occupation. The United States, Britain and France were given Western Germany and West Berlin. The Soviet Union was given Eastern Germany and East Berlin. The Soviet Union felt threatened by the USA's rebuilding of Western Germany and West Berlin.

Reunification

The USA wanted a united, capitalist Germany that it could trade with and would help prevent the spread of communism.

Division

The Soviet Union wanted Germany to be weak, communist and divided, so that it would never be able to attack the Soviet Union again.

Bizonia and Western Germany

☑ It made sense for British and US zones to join together, as it would be easier to administer. The area was called Bizonia and was included in the Marshall Plan. Later on the French zone of occupation was added to create 'West Germany'.

☑ This was *not* popular with the Soviet Union, as Stalin was not consulted. He thought Bizonia went against the agreements made at the Potsdam Conference, and he suspected the USA was aiming to permanently divide richer Western Germany from poorer Eastern Germany.

Eastern Germany and the Berlin Blockade

☑ The Soviet Union had 1.5 million troops in its zone, whereas the Western countries had sent most of their troops home.

☑ Eastern Germany grew almost all the food that West Berlin ate.

☑ Berlin was *deep* in Soviet-controlled Germany, and divided into US, British, French and Soviet zones.

☑ In June 1948 the Soviet Union closed all road, rail and canal links into West Berlin to force British, French and US troops to leave their zone in the city.

☑ The Soviet Union blocked all supplies into Berlin to show it had the power to stop a divided Germany working.

The Berlin Airlift

West Berlin couldn't last for many days without supplies. It looked like the Western powers would have to pull out of Berlin. That would look weak, undermining the USA's image in particular. So Western powers responded with an airlift – between 26 June 1948 and 30 September 1949 thousands of tonnes of supplies were flown daily into Berlin.

West Germany

- The Berlin Airlift made the USA appear peaceful and generous.
- In September 1949, West Germany (FRG) was officially formed, with US support.
- In April 1949, Western European countries and the USA formed NATO to counter the Soviet military threat.

East Germany

- The Berlin Blockade made the Soviet Union appear aggressive and threatening.
- In October 1949, East Germany (GDR) was officially formed.
- In May 1955, the Soviet Union formed the Warsaw Pact to counter the military threat from NATO.

Now try this

1 What were the FRG, GDR and NATO?
2 Explain what happened during the Berlin Blockade and Airlift, 1948–49.

The arms race and the Warsaw Pact

The United States initially had a monopoly of nuclear weapons, but the emergence of the Soviet Union as a nuclear power in 1949 led to the start of the nuclear arms race. The formation of the Warsaw Pact in 1955 further added to Cold War tensions in Europe.

Timeline

The nuclear arms race

1945 USA drops two atomic bombs on Japanese cities.

1949 Soviet Union tests its first atomic bomb.

1952 USA develops H-bomb (hydrogen bomb).

1953 Soviet Union develops H-bomb.

Both superpowers having nuclear weapons was a powerful reason why a cold war did not become a hot war!

The significance of the nuclear arms race

1. Up to 1949, the United States thought it could use its monopoly of nuclear weapons to deter Soviet attack.

2. This meant that US military figures, such as Curtis LeMay and Douglas MacArthur, decided that the best strategy in the event of war with the Soviet Union was to use nuclear weapons.

3. However, by the mid 1950s the development of nuclear weapons to include bigger warheads and missile delivery systems meant that any nuclear war would destroy both sides resulting in Mutually Assured Destruction (MAD).

4. This meant any military confrontation between both sides could rapidly escalate to nuclear war.

5. This meant that the USA and the Soviet Union had to find ways of stopping disputes between them turning into dangerous wars that involved nuclear weapons.

The characteristic mushroom cloud of a nuclear weapons test.

Formation of the Warsaw Pact

☑ The Warsaw Pact was a collective defence treaty involving the Soviet Union, Poland, Hungary, East Germany, Czechoslovakia, Romania, Albania and Bulgaria.

☑ It was set up on 14 May 1955 following West Germany's entry into NATO on 9 May 1955.

Significance of the Warsaw Pact

• The formation of the Warsaw Pact meant there were now two opposing alliances in Europe separated by the Iron Curtain.

• Both alliances planned for military action against the other, including the use of nuclear and conventional weapons.

• The Warsaw Pact gave the Soviet Union direct control over the armed forces of its satellite states, thus strengthening its grip on Eastern Europe.

Now try this

Explain why both the nuclear arms race and the formation of the Warsaw Pact were significant developments during the Cold War.

Soviet control in Hungary

After Stalin died, Soviet leader Khrushchev indicated Soviet control would relax. But when Hungary started to move away from Soviet influence, the Soviet Union tightened its control for fear that if Hungary left the Warsaw Pact, other countries would follow.

Impact of Soviet rule

- 👎 Hungary suffered a lot under Stalin's control.
- 👎 Food and industrial products were shipped off to Russia.
- 👎 Any opposition in Hungary was ruthlessly wiped out.
- 👎 Matyas Rakosi was a brutal ruler. He called himself 'Stalin's best pupil' but was known as the 'Bald Butcher'.
- 👎 Communist rule became very unpopular.

The Hungarian uprising in 1956, showing a statue of Stalin that had been pulled down.

Destalinisation

When Stalin died, Khrushchev took over as Soviet leader. In 1956, in his 'secret speech', Khrushchev hinted that Soviet control would relax.

In October 1956, poor harvests and bread shortages meant that Hungarians started demonstrating against communist control with statues of Stalin pulled down and local communists attacked. Khrushchev appointed a more liberal Prime Minister for Hungary – Imre Nagy – in the hope that the situation would calm down.

Destalinisation meant that the Soviet Union no longer saw itself as a dictatorship. Instead it became a one-party state, governed by the Politburo with Khrushchev as its leader. Many Hungarians mistakenly believed that the end of Stalin's rule would bring an end to communism in Hungary, especially as Soviet troops had already withdrawn from neighbouring Austria.

Nagy as prime minister

Nagy wanted the following reforms for Hungary.

- Leave the Warsaw Pact and become a neutral country.
- Hold free elections leading to no more single-party communist government.
- UN protection from the Soviet Union.

However this was a problem for the Soviet Union because if Nagy succeeded in Hungary other countries in Eastern Europe would follow and the Warsaw Pact would collapse.

Now try this

1. Why were many Hungarians prepared to protest against the government in October 1956?
2. Why was Khrushchev reluctant to support Nagy's reforms of October 1956?

The Soviet invasion of Hungary, 1956

Khrushchev disapproved of Nagy's reforms and in 1956 Soviet troops invaded Hungary. This provoked a strong reaction in the West and in neutral countries condemning the invasion.

The Soviet invasion of Hungary

- Khrushchev disapproved of Nagy's reforms and proposals. If Hungary left the Warsaw Pact, other countries would soon follow.
- Khrushchev worried that Nagy's actions threatened communist rule. He claimed communists were being slaughtered in Hungary. This may have been propaganda, but a number of Hungarian communists had been killed and members of the state security forces, the AVH, attacked in the violence of October 1956, which took place in Budapest and other Hungarian towns and cities. Khrushchev feared the unrest would spread to other satellite states.

- On 4 November 1956, Khrushchev sent 200 000 Soviet troops into Hungary to depose Nagy and restore order.

Damage in Budapest caused by Soviet troops during the invasion of Hungary, 4 November 1956.

The consequences of the Soviet invasion of Hungary

☑ Over 5000 Hungarians were killed as a result of the invasion, and around 1000 Soviet troops. Many Hungarian soldiers loyal to Nagy and the revolution fought against Soviet troops.

☑ Nagy and his government were deposed.

☑ Imre Nagy was arrested, tried and executed. Khrushchev wanted to prevent rebellions in other communist countries, such as Poland, and hoped he could do so by making an example of Nagy.

☑ A new leader, Janos Kadar, was appointed. He introduced the Fifteen Point Programme, which aimed to re-establish communist rule in Hungary. Kadar's policies were more moderate than those of other Soviet satellite states and resulted in Hungary having better living standards than other East European states. Hungarians, aware that the United States was not prepared to help them, grudgingly accepted this modified form of communist rule.

International reaction and consequences

| The United Nations condemned Soviet actions. Some countries boycotted the 1956 Olympics in protest. But stronger actions did not happen. | ⇒ | The USA supported Hungary's uprising – with money, medical aid and words. The USA accepted 80000 refugees from Hungary. | ⇒ | But the USA couldn't send troops: would risk nuclear war. | ⇒ | Hungary was on its own against the Soviet Union: they had to give in. | ⇒ | Satellite states saw that the USA would not defend them against the Soviet Union. Soviet control retightened across Eastern Europe. |

For question 2, think about Khrushchev's concerns, the Soviet invasion, and its consequences.

Now try this

1 Explain **two** consequences of the Hungarian Uprising in 1956.

2 Explain how Khrushchev responded to the Hungarian uprising of 1956.

A divided Berlin

After the war, Germany was divided into four zones and its capital city, Berlin, was also divided into four. The divided city became a focus for the Cold War.

West Berlin

- West Berlin was deep inside Soviet-controlled East Germany.
- Divided Berlin gave the USA a foothold inside the Soviet **Eastern bloc**.
- Some Germans in East Germany did not like having a communist government.
- There were also better jobs with higher wages in the West.
- It was easy to get to West Germany once you had reached the western zones in Berlin.

The refugee problem in Berlin

✓ Between 1949 and 1961, 2.7 million East Germans crossed into West Germany via West Berlin. The population of West Germany increased while the economy benefitted from an influx of skilled workers. Many left for the West, leaving the East with a skills shortage.

✓ This looked bad for the Soviets: people clearly preferred West Germany.

American zone
British zone
French zone
Soviet zone

Division of Berlin

The division of Germany in 1945.

Khrushchev's Berlin ultimatum (November 1958)

- This stated that all Berlin belonged to East Germany and that occupying troops must leave in six months.
- The Soviet Union knew that if it tried to push the West out of Berlin by force, a war would start that it could not win, as the US had more nuclear weapons. So, a series of summit meetings took place between the leaders of the USA and the Soviet Union.

Summit meetings 1959–61 between the USA and the Soviet Union

Summit	Outcome
Geneva (May 1959), involving foreign representatives only	No solution agreed but a further summit organised for Camp David in the USA.
Camp David (Sept 1959), involving Eisenhower and Khrushchev	No solution agreed but a further meeting arranged in Paris.
Paris Summit (May 1960), involving Eisenhower and Khrushchev	A disaster. Khrushchev stormed out because the Soviet Union had shot down a US spy plane over Russia.
Vienna Conference (June 1961), involving Kennedy and Khrushchev	Neither was willing to back down. Khrushchev saw Kennedy's inexperience as a weakness and reissued his ultimatum for the USA to remove its troops from Berlin.

Now try this

1 Explain why West Berlin was so important during the Cold War.
2 Describe the summit meetings that took place between the USA and the Soviet Union over the future of Berlin.

The Cuban Missile Crisis: origins

A revolution in Cuba set it against its neighbour, the USA. The USA attempted to bring Cuba back into its sphere of influence but instead, Castro, Cuba's leader, asked the Soviet Union for help with defence.

The Cuban Revolution, the USA and the Soviet Union

Before 1959 Cuba was very closely linked to the USA, for example, there were lots of US-owned businesses. Cuba had a socialist revolution in 1959 and the USA refused to deal with the new government. Instead, Cuba started to build **economic links** with the Soviet Union, for example, trading Soviet oil for Cuban sugar. The relationship between Cuba and the USA deteriorated.

Get Castro!

- The USA refused to recognise Castro's government because it did not want a socialist country in their sphere of influence, especially not a country with close links to the Soviet Union.
- The CIA tried to assassinate the leader of Cuba, Fidel Castro, with no success.
- The CIA convinced President Kennedy that a US-backed invasion of Cuba, designed to overthrow Castro, could solve the problem.

Fidel Castro

The Bay of Pigs incident – 17 April 1961

What the CIA told Kennedy:

- 👍 The invasion will look like a Cuban revolt – we've trained Cuban exiles and disguised old US planes as Cuban.
- 👍 Castro's control of Cuba is very weak.
- 👍 Most Cubans hate Castro.

What actually happened:

- 👎 The planes were recognised as US planes and photographed, and the information was published. The world knew that the USA had backed the invasion.
- 👎 In fact, Castro knew of the invasion in advance and 1400 US-backed troops met 20 000 of Castro's troops. The US-backed troops surrendered.
- 👎 In fact, most Cubans did not want their old leader, Batista, back again, because he had been corrupt.

The impact:

- Ended all chances of a friendly USA-Cuba relationship.
- Castro announced that he was a communist.
- Cuba and the Soviet Union started building closer ties – including military defence for Cuba...

Now try this

1. Describe the Bay of Pigs incident in your own words. What did President Kennedy think would happen and why did it fail?
2. Explain **two** effects of the Bay of Pigs invasion.
3. Why did the USA seek to overthrow Castro?

Czechoslovakia and the Prague Spring

Like in Hungary, a relaxation of control in Czechoslovakia – another satellite state – led to a challenge to Soviet authority.

The impact of Soviet rule on Czechoslovakia

- Czechoslovakia's economy and living standards declined.
- Any opposition to communism was crushed.
- Communist rule became very unpopular.

Alexander Dubček

- In January 1968 Dubček became the Czechoslovakian leader.
- He was a good friend of Soviet leader Leonid Brezhnev.
- He was a communist and supporter of the Warsaw Pact but wanted to make communism better and easier to live under. Dubček called this 'socialism with a human face'.
- His reforms resulted in the 'Prague Spring' – a period of increased political freedom – in April 1968 and lots of criticism of communism resulted.

Brezhnev and Dubček

Dubček's reforms

Relaxation of censorship meant more freedom to say and write things, even if critical of communism.
More democracy allowed other parties alongside the Communist Party.
More power was given to the Czechoslovakian parliament and Soviet control was reduced. The economy was also reformed with 'market socialism' allowing for the introduction of some 'capitalist elements'.
The powers of the secret police were also reduced.

How Czechoslovaks responded

Students, intellectuals, workers and young members of the Communist Party of Czechoslovakia welcomed Dubček's reforms enthusiastically. The reforms also led to writers, such as Vaclav Havel and Milan Kundera, writing books that were highly critical of Soviet-style communism.

Not all Czechoslovaks were happy: members of the secret police and some senior army officers resented losing their power and status due to the reforms.

How the rest of the communist world responded

- ✓ The Prague Spring horrified many older Czechoslovakian communists, as they felt it would lead to the collapse of communism in Czechoslovakia.
- ✓ Brezhnev and other communists in Eastern Europe, such as Eric Honecker, the leader of East Germany, were especially concerned. They feared the Prague Spring would lead to demands for reform elsewhere in the Eastern bloc that would threaten communist rule in Eastern Europe.
- ✓ Brezhnev now had a dilemma: Dubček was a friend and military action would damage the Soviet Union's reputation. On the other hand, if he did nothing, expectations would rise and the whole Eastern bloc might collapse.

Now try this

1 Explain how Dubček wished to reform communism in Czechoslovakia in 1968.
2 Why did people react to the Prague Spring in different ways?

Consider the reactions of ordinary Czechoslovaks and those of traditional communists.

The construction of the Berlin Wall

The Soviet Union and USA started negotiations to sort out the Berlin problem, but they broke down. Khrushchev's solution was the Berlin Wall.

Building the Berlin Wall

- The four summit meetings of 1959–61 had failed to resolve the problem in Berlin, and President Kennedy started to prepare the USA for nuclear war.

- Khrushchev could not risk a nuclear war with the United States, but he still needed to solve the refugee problem that existed in Berlin.

- His solution was to build the Berlin Wall in August 1961. This was designed to prevent East Berliners travelling to West Berlin. In future, any East Berliner travelling to West Berlin would be shot.

- On 12 August 1961, East German troops erected a barbed wire fence around West Berlin. The fence eventually became a heavily guarded wall. Soviet tanks were deployed to stop Western access to the East. By the end of October 1961, West Berlin was completely cut off from East Germany.

Building the Berlin Wall August 1961. Note the number of soldiers in the background. Over 200 East Germans were shot trying to cross the wall between 1961 and 1989.

Why the Berlin Wall was built

1. Khrushchev backed down: as he knew he couldn't win a nuclear war.

2. Despite the Berlin ultimatum, the Western powers stayed in Berlin.

Do not confuse the Berlin Wall Crisis with the Berlin Blockade.

3. Instead, the Berlin Wall was built (from August 1961).

4. Anyone trying to escape was shot at. Many people were killed.

5. The wall stopped East Germans leaving for the West, which solved the crisis.

6. This way, Khrushchev avoided war with USA but still looked strong.

Now try this

1. Write a narrative explaining the events that led to the construction of the Berlin Wall between 1958 and 1961.

For a narrative answer, begin with the refugee problem, move on to the failure of the summits and finish with the construction of the Wall.

2. Why did Khrushchev reach the decision to construct the Berlin Wall in August 1961?

To answer this 'why' question, you need to look at the reasons why the Wall was constructed.

The events of the Cuban Missile Crisis

When the USA discovered the Soviet Union's missile sites on Cuba, the USA was torn on how best to respond: attack while it could or do everything possible to avoid war.

The Cuban missile sites

The Soviet Union saw Cuba as a fix to a key strategic problem: the USA had missiles close to the Soviet Union (e.g. in the UK), but the Soviet Union had no missiles close to the USA.

Cuba saw Soviet missiles as a great way to prevent the USA from invading Cuba again.

In September 1962, Soviet ships carried nuclear warheads and missiles to Cuba.

Then in October 1962, US spy planes photographed the Cuban missile sites and the secret was out.

The US public learned that they were now in range of Soviet nuclear missiles. There was panic.

MEDIUM RANGE BALLISTIC MISSILE BASE IN CUBA
SAN CRISTOBAL

How should the USA respond?

President Kennedy and his team thought through the different options. Some advisers (the '**hawks**') wanted to attack straight away, while others (the '**doves**') wanted to avoid nuclear war if at all possible.

Ignore the Cuban missiles: the USA also had many missile bases close to the Soviet Union, for example, in Turkey.

Do a deal and get the Soviet Union to withdraw from Cuba in return for the USA withdrawing from one of its missile bases close to the Soviet Union.

Invade Cuba: US troops would invade and get rid of the Castro government.

Nuclear attack: attack the Soviet Union quickly before the Soviet Union could attack the USA.

Warn Castro that his actions put Cuba in grave danger and hope that Castro would decide to stop the missile site construction.

Blockade Cuba to stop any more missiles or equipment coming from the Soviet Union.

Destroy Cuban missile sites. This could be done with airstrikes and so wouldn't need nuclear strikes or a land invasion.

Now try this

If you were an adviser to President Kennedy, which option would you have recommended and why?

← Remember to link your recommendation to the arms race!

The Brezhnev Doctrine and Soviet control in Czechoslovakia

Brezhnev could not accept Dubček's reforms and the Soviet Union invaded Czechoslovakia in August 1968. Brezhnev then established the Brezhnev Doctrine.

Brezhnev's response to Dubček's reforms

✓ Brezhnev could not allow the reforms, as any weakness in control could mean the break-up of the Warsaw Pact – even though this wasn't Dubček's intention.

✓ Brezhnev failed to convince Dubček to stop the reforms.

✓ In August 1968, the Soviet Union sent tanks to Prague and Dubček was arrested.

✓ Czechoslovakia returned to being under strict Soviet control under Gustav Husak. This was known as 'normalisation'.

The Soviet invasion of Czechoslovakia, August 1968.

Consequences of the Brezhnev Doctrine

| From now on, the Soviet Union declared the right to invade any Eastern bloc country that was threatening the security of the Eastern bloc as a whole. | → | The USA condemned the invasion but did nothing to stop it: it feared war. | → | Western European communist parties were horrified and declared themselves independent from the Soviet Communist Party. | → | Yugoslavia and Romania also backed off from the Soviet Union, weakening the Soviet Union's grip on Eastern Europe. |

The importance of the Soviet invasion of Czechoslovakia

The Soviet invasion of Czechoslovakia was important because the Brezhnev Doctrine meant that the Soviet Union reserved the right to invade any country that threatened the security of the Eastern bloc. Therefore, other East European states, such as Poland or Hungary, were required to rigidly stick to Soviet-style communism or risk invasion themselves.

Now try this

1 Draw up a timeline showing the key events in the Cold War 1957–68.

2 Explain **two** effects of the Soviet invasion of Czechoslovakia.

3 Explain why the Soviet invasion of Czechoslovakia was important to Soviet control of Eastern Europe.

Remember to think about the different places where events took place and the actions of the USA and Soviet Union.

The Berlin Wall and US–Soviet relations

While the construction of the Berlin Wall affected relations between the Soviet Union and the United States, it made war over Berlin less likely. Following President Kennedy's visit in 1963, West Berlin became an enduring symbol of freedom during the Cold War.

The impact of the Wall

- ✓ After the Berlin Wall went up in 1961, Western (British, US and French) troops remained in Berlin.

- ✓ The Wall solved the refugee problem, as East Germans could no longer travel to West Germany.

- ✓ The number of military alerts in Berlin declined as a result of the construction of the Wall. President Kennedy commented that, although not a nice solution, a wall was at least better than a war. The Wall seemed to suggest that the Soviets were no longer interested in unifying Berlin under communist rule, as Khrushchev had originally demanded in November 1958.

- ✓ The Wall was a humiliation for the Soviet Union and a propaganda victory for the West, as it suggested that East Germans preferred living in capitalist West Germany and had to be forced to stay in communist East Germany.

- ✓ The Wall was a notorious barrier between the freedoms enjoyed by West Berliners and those denied to East Berliners. It meant West Berlin became an enduring symbol of freedom. This was highlighted further by the fact that over 200 people lost their lives trying to cross the Wall.

- ✓ Khrushchev mistakenly thought that Kennedy had shown weakness by allowing the Wall to be built, and this encouraged him to think about deploying missiles in Cuba.

Kennedy's visit to West Berlin, 1963

- Kennedy famously visited West Berlin in 1963 and claimed "Ich bin ein Berliner" ("I am a Berliner").

- His speech was an expression of solidarity with the people of West Berlin. The fact that Kennedy chose to visit West Berlin personally and give this speech demonstrated that the United States and NATO were prepared to defend West Berlin from communist attack.

- Kennedy was also speaking after the Cuban Missile Crisis had ended and was showing his audience – both German and American – that he was not 'soft on communism'.

Kennedy speaking in West Berlin, 26 June 1963. West German leaders had previously shown him the Wall.

The Iron Curtain divides East and West

The construction of the Berlin Wall filled the last remaining gap in the Iron Curtain and meant that Europe was now completely divided.

There were two Germanys.

There were two different ideologies (capitalism and communism).

On either side of the Iron Curtain

There were two different alliances (NATO and the Warsaw Pact).

Now try this

1 Explain two consequences of the construction of the Berlin Wall in 1961.

2 Explain the significance of Kennedy's Berlin speech of 26 June 1963.

 Look again at the picture and notes on this page.

The consequences of the Cuban Missile Crisis

During the Cuban Missile Crisis the world came very close to nuclear war. There was a need to ensure this did not happen again, so relations between the United States and the Soviet Union actually improved after the crisis, leading to a period of cooling tensions, known as **détente**.

Short-term consequences of the crisis

- Communist Cuba survived as Kennedy gave assurances the USA would not invade Cuba again.
- The Soviet Union looked weak, as the world did not know the USA had removed missiles from Turkey. This undermined Khrushchev and Brezhnev replaced him as Soviet leader in 1964.
- US 'doves' came out well, as their desire to avoid war resulted in the missiles being withdrawn.

Timeline

1962

16 Oct President Kennedy is informed that US spy planes have found missile sites on Cuba.

22 Oct Kennedy decides against an attack. Orders a blockade of Cuba.

24 Oct One Soviet oil tanker is allowed through blockade, but the other Soviet ships stop before the blockade and turn around.

25 Oct USA and Soviet Union prepare for immediate nuclear attack.

26-27 Oct Cuba gets ready for invasion.
Khrushchev offers to remove missiles from Cuba if USA does the same from its Italy and Turkey bases.
A US spy plane is shot down over Cuba. US 'hawks' demand retaliation.
Robert Kennedy sets up a deal in which the USA would secretly withdraw warheads from Italy and Turkey.

28 Oct Khrushchev agrees to the deal: missiles withdrawn in return for USA agreeing never to attack Cuba and taking its missiles out of Italy and Turkey.

Long-term consequences

The Cuban Missile Crisis showed how easily a nuclear war could start. The USA initiated a move to **détente** – a less stressful, more informed relationship between the USA and the Soviet Union.

- The Hotline Agreement created a direct communication link between Washington and Moscow.
- Limited Test Ban Treaty (August 1963) – both sides agreed to ban all nuclear weapon testing except for underground tests.
- In 1963 Kennedy gave a speech about working with the Soviet Union to focus on their 'common interests'.
- However, the Soviet Union was determined to catch up with USA in the arms race and achieved this by 1965. This meant Mutually Assured Destruction (MAD). War would be so terrible that it must be avoided at all costs.
- The USA and the Soviet Union also signed the Outer Space Treaty in 1967, which banned the deployment of nuclear weapons in space, and the Nuclear Non-Proliferation Treaty in 1968, which was an agreement not to share their nuclear technology with other countries.

Make sure you are clear about the chronology of the Cuban Missile Crisis.

Now try this

1. Explain how the USA responded to the discovery of missiles in Cuba.
2. Explain **two** consequences of the Cuban Missile Crisis.

*Remember: only focus on what the USA did **after** the missiles were discovered.*

International reaction to Soviet measures in Czechoslovakia

The Soviet response to the Prague Spring brought about a mixed reaction in both the East and the West. It did not damage the growing détente between East and West.

Impact on the West

- ✓ The United States and West Germany condemned the invasion and the Brezhnev Doctrine that followed it. The Soviet invasion was even described as 'the rape of Czechoslovakia'.
- ✓ However, the USA and West Germany offered no military support or assistance. The United States was already bogged down in the Vietnam War and also did not want to provoke an international crisis.
- ✓ Communist leaders, such as Jacques Duclos in France and Enrico Berlinguer in Italy, were appalled by the invasion, France and Italy therefore began to end their links with the Soviet Union.

Impact on the East

- ✓ The invasion and the Brezhnev Doctrine limited reforms in other Eastern bloc countries who feared a Soviet invasion.
- ✓ Countries such as Poland pursued policies that ignored public opinion, which increasingly demanded change. This led to public protests.
- ✓ The invasion strengthened Soviet control over the Eastern bloc as they could use military force to ensure their dominance.
- ✓ Yet the crisis also exposed differences in the Eastern bloc. Both Romania (led by Nicolae Ceauşescu) and Yugoslavia (led by Josip Broz Tito) condemned the invasion and signed alliances with communist China, dividing the communist world.

Jacque Duclos, leader of the French Communist Party. The Party originally had links with the Soviet Union but dropped them after the Soviet invasion of Czechoslovakia.

Josip Broz Tito, communist leader of Yugoslavia. Yugoslavia was a communist state that was not a member of the Warsaw Pact.

Soviet influence within the West began to decline as Western communist leaders developed a form of communism different to that in the Soviet Union.

Impact on superpower relations

- The Soviet invasion of Czechoslovakia did little to damage the growing détente between East and West. This was helped by the fact that relatively few people (less than 100) died as a result of the invasion.

- However, the invasion did create a sense of complacency in Brezhnev's mind. He believed that any Soviet military intervention in areas that contained pro-Soviet governments would not be challenged by the United States. This view proved to be mistaken following the Soviet invasion of Afghanistan in 1979.

Now try this

Explain how international relations were affected by the Soviet invasion of Czechoslovakia.

 You can focus here on either superpower relations or the impact of the invasion on the East and the West.

Détente in the 1970s

Détente, meaning the relaxing of tension between rivals, was used to describe the relationship between the USA and the Soviet Union in the later 1960s and 1970s.

SALT 1 – Strategic Arms Limitation Treaty (1972)

Superpowers agreed to limit the number of nuclear weapons they had.

✓ No further production of strategic ballistic weapons (short-range, lightweight missiles).

✓ No increase in number of intercontinental ballistic weapons (ICBMs) (though new ones could be added to replace old ones).

✓ No new nuclear missile launchers. New submarines that could launch nuclear weapons (SLBMs) only allowed as replacements for existing missile launchers.

✓ The Anti-Ballistic Missile (ABM) Treaty limited both sides to two ABM deployment areas.

How effective was SALT 1?

👍 Slowed down the arms race by placing limits on the number of bombers, ICBMs and SLBMs each side could have.

👍 Led to further negotiations that culminated in the SALT 2 Treaty in 1979.

👍 Ensured that neither side had a decisive advantage in strategic nuclear weapons.

👎 Did not cover intermediate nuclear weapons, which both sides continued to deploy in Europe during the late 1970s.

Détente had limits. Superpowers still targeted nuclear weapons at each other and competed for influence. Also, the Soviet Union didn't honour the human rights agreements from the Helsinki Agreements.

1975 Helsinki Conference

The Helsinki Agreements were signed in Helsinki, Finland, in 1975, by all European countries except Albania and Andorra, as well as the USA, the Soviet Union and Canada. Representatives from 35 countries agreed on security issues, cooperation, human rights and borders.

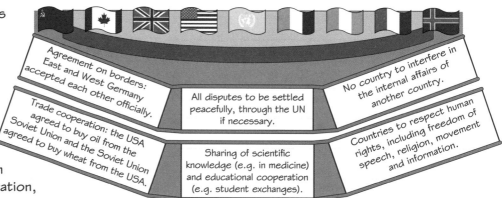

Agreement on borders: East and West Germany accepted each other officially.

Trade cooperation: the USA agreed to buy oil from the Soviet Union and the Soviet Union agreed to buy wheat from the USA.

All disputes to be settled peacefully, through the UN if necessary.

Sharing of scientific knowledge (e.g. in medicine) and educational cooperation (e.g. student exchanges).

No country to interfere in the internal affairs of another country.

Countries to respect human rights, including freedom of speech, religion, movement and information.

The importance of Helsinki

* Helped the USA and the Soviet Union form a stable relationship.
* Represented the high point of détente.
* Coincided with more US-Soviet cooperation, like the Apollo-Soyuz Test Project (1975) – a joint space mission – and trade agreements.

Limits to Helsinki

* The Soviet Union continued to focus on Eastern bloc countries and to apply the Brezhnev Doctrine. It treated dissidents (protesters) harshly; scientist Alexander Sakharov was arrested, hospitalised and force-fed.
* The USA continued to prioritise its interests in countries it could influence, like Chile and El Salvador.

Now try this

1 Explain two consequences of détente.

2 What was the importance of SALT 1 for the development of superpower relations?

3 Explain why the Helsinki Agreements were important in improving relations between the USA and the Soviet Union.

SALT 2 and the failure of détente

SALT 2 was an arms control agreement that marked the end of détente. The treaty was never ratified due to the Soviet invasion of Afghanistan in 1979.

SALT 2 – Strategic Arms Limitation Treaty (1979)

✓ Under negotiation since 1972.

✓ Based on the Vladivostok Accords (1974) – agreements between US and Soviet governments.

✓ Soviet leader Leonid Brezhnev and US President Jimmy Carter signed the agreement in Vienna in June 1979.

✓ Each superpower limited to 2250 warheads. SALT 2 counted warheads while SALT 1 simply counted missiles and bombers.

✓ Imposed limits on new launch systems including multi-warhead missiles.

Why SALT 2 failed

- Some West German politicians opposed the treaty, as they feared it weakened the defence of West Germany. They thought that, after the treaty, the USA would be less likely to use its nuclear weapons if West Germany was attacked by the Soviet Union.

- Some US politicians thought the treaty made too many concessions to the Soviet Union.

- US–Soviet relations soured after the Soviet invasion of Afghanistan in 1979. This meant the US Senate never ratified (approved) the treaty, so it never became official US policy.

Turn to pages 24 and 25 for details of the Soviet invasion of Afghanistan and its impact.

How successful were SALT 1 and SALT 2?

Arms control agreements only set out to limit the number of warheads each superpower had. They did not attempt to reduce them.	→ Arms control agreements placed limits on the number of anti-ballistic missiles (ABMs), intercontinental ballistic weapons (ICBMs), nuclear weapons (SLBMs) and long-range bombers each side had.	→ This reduced the possibility of nuclear war by ensuring that neither side had a first strike capacity (the ability to destroy all the other side's nuclear weapons in one strike). This made sure a system of nuclear deterrence remained.

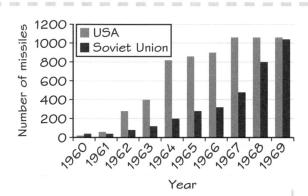

The Inter Continental Ballistic Missile (ICBM) Build Up 1960–69. ICBMs were missiles that left the earth's atmosphere before re-entering it to reach their targets.

Nuclear deterrence occurs when the possibility of a response with nuclear weapons prevents the other side from acting aggressively. British Prime Minister Margaret Thatcher argued that nuclear weapons kept the peace in Europe and the world.

Remember: nuclear weapons were becoming increasingly expensive by the mid 1970s. The Soviet Union's economy was weaker than the United States', and so the Soviet Union found it increasingly difficult to keep up in the arms race.

Now try this

Explain two features of the SALT 2 Treaty.

21

Changing attitudes

Ronald Reagan became US president in 1981. He believed that the USA had a mission from God to win the Cold War.

In 1985, Mikhail Gorbachev became leader of the Soviet Union. He recognised that the Soviet Union could not win the Cold War. Together, Gorbachev and Reagan would bring the Cold War to an end within a few years.

Reagan and the 'Evil Empire'

After he was first elected, President Reagan made no efforts to get détente up and running again.

- In fact, he described the Soviet Union as an 'Evil Empire' – this was not diplomatic!
- He kick-started the arms race again.
- US technology was developing fast in the 1980s, especially computing.
- The USA poured money into developing new missile technology.

Crisis in the Soviet Union

The Soviet Union could not keep up with the USA.

- Its economy was in poor shape, partly because it spent so much on weapons.
- Living standards were very low right across the Eastern bloc.
- It was bogged down in the war in Afghanistan.
- The Soviet Union did not have the USA's computing expertise.
- The Soviet Union could not keep pace with the USA's new missile technology.

Geneva, November 1985

- Gorbachev and Reagan met at the Geneva summit.
- The two men got on well and agreed to more meetings.

Gorbachev and Reagan meet for the first time in Geneva, 1985.

Reagan's change of heart

- ✓ Public opinion was against the arms race, especially in Europe.
- ✓ Gorbachev was popular. There was 'Gorbymania' in Western Europe and even in the United States.
- ✓ Reagan liked Gorbachev and was prepared to work with him to improve US–Soviet relations. Margaret Thatcher, the British Prime Minister and a close ally of President Reagan, described Gorbachev as a man she could do business with.

The significance of Gorbachev's and Reagan's changing attitudes

- ✓ They represented an easing of Cold War tensions.
- ✓ Led to greater cooperation between the USA and the Soviet Union.
- ✓ Led to arms control agreements, the INF Treaty and START I.

Turn to page 23 for details of the INF Treaty and turn to page 28 for details of START I.

Now try this

Explain how relations between the USA and the Soviet Union improved between 1985 and 1987.

New thinking and the INF Treaty

In 1985, Mikhail Gorbachev became leader of the Soviet Union – he was to be its last leader. Gorbachev tried to reform the Soviet Union in order to solve its economic, social and political problems. He rejected any argument that this meant capitalism had won: he felt he was making socialism stronger.

Gorbachev as leader

Recognised that the economy was failing.

Recognised that the Soviet people were unhappy and distrustful of government.

Brought in *perestroika* (restructuring). It meant new ways of doing things.

Brought in *glasnost* (openness). It meant more freedom for people to say what they really thought.

Foreign relations changed – more open and positive.

Desperate to get the Soviet Union out of the war in Afghanistan.

Was very slow to allow democratic elections in Soviet Union.

Tried to cover up the scale of the massive nuclear accident at Chernobyl.

Did not want capitalism, just a stronger socialism.

Never planned to cause end of Soviet Union.

Mikhail Gorbachev

Reykjavik, October 1986

- Reagan and Gorbachev said they would work to cut down the number of nuclear weapons they had.
- Gorbachev wanted an end to Reagan's Strategic Defence Initiative (SDI) – Reagan's plan to have satellites in space to destroy nuclear missiles. However, Reagan didn't agree to this.

Turn to page 26 to find out more about Reagan's Strategic Defence Initiative (SDI) – also known as 'Star Wars'.

INF Treaty, December 1987

- Diplomats continued the discussions from Reykjavik and came up with the INF Treaty, signed in Washington.
- INF stood for Intermediate-Range Nuclear Forces – nuclear weapons with a 500–5500 km range.
- The INF Treaty got rid of all 500–5500 km nuclear missiles each superpower had – better than SALT 1.
- The INF Treaty largely applied in Europe, where most of these missiles were deployed.

Now try this

Why were the changing attitudes of Reagan and Gorbachev important in improving superpower relations?

The significance of the Soviet invasion of Afghanistan

Brezhnev gambled that the USA wouldn't do anything if the Soviet Union clamped down on trouble in Afghanistan. But the US reaction revived the Cold War and put an end to détente.

Background

In 1968 the Soviet Union sent tanks into Czechoslovakia to put down the Prague Spring. The USA condemned this, but didn't do anything.

In 1979, the Soviet Union sent troops into Afghanistan, a country with a communist government, to take control after the president was assassinated. This time the USA reacted very strongly.

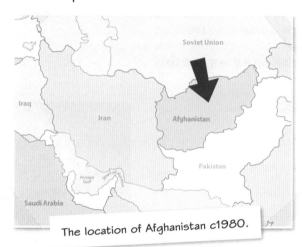

The location of Afghanistan c1980.

The Soviet invasion of Afghanistan

The Soviet Union saw Afghanistan as in its sphere of influence, as it was bordering the Soviet Union. This meant President Taraki's government had to be communist and Soviet-backed.

When President Taraki was assassinated during civil war and replaced by Hafizullah Amin, the Soviet Union felt its influence in Afghanistan was threatened.

Brezhnev ordered Soviet troops to invade Afghanistan in December 1979. Barbrak Karmal was made president and Amin and many of his supporters were killed.

Brezhnev believed wrongly that the USA and its president, Jimmy Carter, would not object to the invasion.

Soviet troops had to remain in the country to keep Karmal in power. Afghan rebels known as the Mujahideen resisted these troops.

Why was Carter worried?

☑ The USA was worried that the Soviet Union would get more control in the Middle East.

☑ A successful invasion of Afghanistan might mean Soviet influence in Iran.

☑ Iran could block Middle East oil exports at the Straits of Hormuz. Middle East oil was essential to the USA's prosperity.

Now try this

Explain how the Soviet Union involved itself in Afghanistan in 1979.

Your answer should be no more than 2–3 paragraphs long and should focus on the sequence of events that led to the Soviet invasion of Afghanistan.

The consequences of the Soviet invasion of Afghanistan

The Soviet invasion of Afghanistan marked the end of détente and the start of the 'Second Cold War' between the superpowers. It led to the Carter Doctrine and the Olympic boycotts of 1980 and 1984.

The Carter Doctrine, January 1980

US President Jimmy Carter took the following actions:

- ✓ He threatened to use force if the Soviet Union attempted to take control of the Persian Gulf.
- ✓ The USA imposed economic sanctions – there would be no trade with the Soviet Union. This meant the USA would no longer export grain to or import oil from the Soviet Union.
- ✓ The USA and its allies, Saudi Arabia and Pakistan, secretly provided assistance to the Mujahideen. This meant the USA and its allies were directly backing a war against the Soviet Union in Afghanistan.
- ✓ In this way the USA ceased cooperating with the Soviet Union and began to confront it instead.

The end of SALT 2

In 1980 the USA broke off diplomatic relations with the Soviet Union and the US Senate refused to sign SALT 2, which had been signed by Carter and Brezhnev in 1979.

- The US began to build up its own conventional and nuclear weapons. It began to develop cruise and Pershing missiles for deployment in Europe.
- The Soviets responded by developing their own medium range weapon, the SS20 missile.

In this way the US–Soviet arms race began to speed up again, as more nuclear weapons were produced and deployed.

The Mujahideen was made up of the Afghan militias opposed to the Soviet occupation.

The Olympic boycotts

The USA **boycotted** the 1980 Olympic Games in Moscow in retaliation for the Soviet invasion of Afghanistan.

In retaliation for the US boycott of the Moscow Olympics, the Soviet Union boycotted the 1984 Olympic Games in Los Angeles.

This brought to an end the cooperation and sporting competition between the USA and the Soviet Union that characterised détente.

The opening ceremony of the 1980 Olympic Games in Moscow.

Further consequences of the Soviet invasion of Afghanistan

The USA:

- The Soviet invasion of Afghanistan persuaded many Americans that the Soviet Union could not be trusted.
- This helped lead to the election of President Reagan in November 1980. He was an anti-communist with a hard-line (tough) attitude towards the Soviet Union.

The Soviet Union:

- Soviet Union troops remained in Afghanistan, to keep Barbrak Karmal in power.
- These troops came under repeated attack from the Mujahideen, leading to rising casualties on both sides.
- Pressure was put on the Soviet leadership to end the increasingly unpopular war.

Now try this

1 Explain **two** consequences of the war in Afghanistan.
2 Why was the Soviet invasion of Afghanistan so important to US–Soviet relations?

Consider the consequences of the Soviet invasion of Afghanistan and how relations between the USA and the Soviet Union got worse.

Reagan and the 'Second Cold War'

Between 1979 and 1984, following the Soviet invasion of Afghanistan, relations between the USA and the Soviet Union deteriorated in what was known as the 'Second Cold War'. Ronald Reagan became US president in 1981. He believed the USA had a 'mission from God' to win the Cold War.

The United States

☑ Had recovered after its defeat in the Vietnam War, where it had failed to stop the spread of communism.

☑ Was beginning to develop information technology, especially computers.

☑ Was becoming increasingly determined to stop and even roll back communism.

☑ Was prepared to fund anti-communist forces in Central America and Southern Africa.

The Soviet Union

☑ Was in decline, with poor living standards.

☑ Had an ageing leadership. Brezhnev died in 1982 to be replaced by Andropov and then Chernyenko. All three leaders were over 70.

☑ Had ageing technology in an economy that was only 20 per cent the size of the US economy.

☑ Was struggling to deal with anti-communist protest in Eastern Europe, especially in Poland where the trade union 'Solidarity' was demanding reforms.

US–Soviet relations deteriorate

Between 1979 and 1984, relations between the United States and the Soviet Union declined due to:

For more on the Olympic boycotts of 1980 and 1984, go to page 25.

- the Olympic boycotts (1980 and 1984)
- the election of President Reagan, who was very anti-communist
- increased military expenditure on missiles and the USA's Strategic Defence Initiative (SDI); the Soviet Union retaliated but could not keep up with the United States, as its economy was much smaller
- the on-going war following the Soviet invasion of Afghanistan
- the breakdown of the SALT 2 arms control negotiations
- the shooting down of KAL007 in September 1983.

The shooting down of KAL007, a South Korean airliner, by Soviet fighters (who claimed it had violated Soviet airspace) amounted to the lowest point of the 'Second Cold War'. A number of Americans were killed and the USA roundly condemned the attack.

Reagan's Strategic Defence Initiative (SDI)

Previously, nuclear strategy was based on **MAD**. If the USA and Soviet Union would destroy each other (and everyone else) in a nuclear war, it was too risky to start one.

But President Reagan wanted to win the Cold War, so he launched SDI, known as 'Star Wars', in March 1983. SDI was a plan to have satellites, lasers and mirrors in space that would destroy Soviet intercontinental nuclear missiles before they reached the USA.

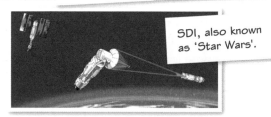

SDI, also known as 'Star Wars'.

'Star Wars' badly damaged East–West relations. The Soviet Union argued it broke the 1967 Outer Space Treaty and gave the USA a decisive advantage in the arms race. In December 1983, Soviet negotiators walked out of the arms control talks in Geneva.

Now try this

1 In what ways did US–Soviet relations decline during the 'Second Cold War'?

Consider the different ways the relationship declined: the arms race, diplomatically, economically.

2 Explain two effects of the Strategic Defence Initiative.

Consider the effects of SDI: did it make US–Soviet relations better or worse?

The loosening Soviet grip on Eastern Europe

Gorbachev's reforms spread out from the Soviet Union to Eastern bloc countries, but not quite how he intended. Instead of making the Soviet system work better, the countries of the Eastern bloc and many of the republics of the Soviet Union wanted to become independent.

Brezhnev

Whenever something in an Eastern bloc country makes it turn towards capitalism, the rest of the Eastern bloc must make it turn back to communism.

Eastern bloc countries should be free to run themselves how they want and the Soviet Union will not stop them.

Gorbachev

Gorbachev scrapped the Brezhnev Doctrine because:

☑ He believed openness would make all Eastern bloc countries better.

☑ The Eastern bloc communist governments were only planning a little reform.

☑ Reform would end unrest in countries such as Poland, where the trade union Solidarity and the Roman Catholic Church had challenged the government.

☑ The Soviet Union had to improve trade relations with the West to rebuild its economy. The West would only improve trade if repression was reduced.

☑ Cost of troops and military hardware was crippling the Soviet Union's economy. It could no longer afford to maintain the Warsaw Pact.

Timeline

Dec 1988 Gorbachev announces the end of the Brezhnev Doctrine.

Aug 1989 Hungary opens its borders to East Germans.

Oct 1989 Gorbachev announces that Eastern bloc states can go their own way.

Nov 1989 Fall of the Berlin Wall.

Dec 1989 Communist governments fall in Czechoslovakia, Bulgaria and Romania.

The break up of the Eastern bloc

In December 1988, Gorbachev announced that ideology should play a smaller role in foreign affairs. This meant that Soviet troops would no longer intervene in Eastern Europe to support communism.

Gorbachev's announcement weakened the communist governments in Eastern Europe, resulting in many revolutions between 1989 and 1990 (see timeline above). Of all these revolutions only the Romanian revolution was violent.

In all the old Eastern bloc countries non-communist governments now came to power.

Now try this

Explain how Soviet control of Eastern Europe ended between 1989 and 1990.

The fall of the Berlin Wall

The fall of the Berlin Wall in November 1989 led to the reunification of Germany and the end of Soviet control in Eastern Europe.

The fall of the Berlin Wall

- Since the summer of 1989 demands for change had been building in East Germany, resulting in public demonstrations in many East German cities, especially Leipzig.
- The East German leader, Eric Honecker, received no assurances from Mikhail Gorbachev that he would support any attempt to deal with these protests using force. Honecker resigned and was replaced by the more moderate Egon Krenz.
- The growth of democracy in Hungary meant that East Germans could now travel to West Germany through Czechoslovakia and Hungary.
- On 9 November the East German government announced that East Germans could now travel to West Germany.
- Crowds of jubilant East and West Germans now began to chip away at the wall leading to its collapse.

A citizen celebrates on top of the Berlin Wall, 10 November 1989.

The significance of the fall of the Berlin Wall for Germany

- German reunification: East Germany ceased to exist and became part of a united Germany in 1990, with Berlin as its capital.
- The Soviet Union withdrew its troops from what was East Germany.
- British, French and US troops remained in western Germany.

The significance of the fall of the Berlin Wall for superpower relations

- The end of the Warsaw Pact in July 1991.
- The withdrawal of Soviet troops from Eastern Europe from 1990 onwards.
- NATO continued to exist but expanded to include many former members of the Warsaw Pact including Poland and Hungary.
- The fall of the Berlin Wall gave further momentum to the 'thaw' in the Cold War.
- The Conventional Forces in Europe (CFE) Agreement (1990) set limits on non-nuclear forces deployed in Europe.
- At the Strategic Arms Reduction Treaty (START) (1991), the USA and Soviet Union agreed to reduce nuclear warheads by about a third, with an additional undertaking to reduce them further.

Now try this

This answer requires you to explain **two** effects of the fall of the Berlin Wall. Use the list of points above to help you do this.

1 Explain two effects of the fall of the Berlin Wall.
2 Explain how Soviet influence in Eastern Europe declined between 1989 and 1990.

The end of the Cold War

The break-up of the Eastern bloc was followed by the break-up of the Soviet Union. In December 1991, Gorbachev dissolved the Soviet Union and resigned. The Cold War had ended.

The break-up of the Soviet Union

Gorbachev's **glasnost** policies meant people could say what they thought, but **perestroika** only made the Soviet economy worse. This meant that living conditions for everyone got even worse than before. Many Soviet republics began to demand independence in 1990–91.

Growing opposition to Gorbachev

* *Perestroika* and *glasnost* were not working and the economy was performing poorly.
* Many of the republics, such as Estonia, Latvia and Lithuania (the Baltic States), wanted to leave the Soviet Union.
* Some army officers felt that Gorbachev had betrayed communism. In August 1991 they launched a failed military takeover (or coup) against him.

To remind yourself of Gorbachev's policies of glasnost and perestroika, go to page 23.

The end of communism in the Soviet Union

* Gorbachev tried to save Soviet communism by issuing a new constitution in the Soviet Union that would have given Soviet republics, such as Estonia, Latvia, Lithuania and Ukraine, more independence. However, the leaders of these countries wanted even greater independence and rejected the constitution.
* As a result, on 25 December 1991, Gorbachev announced the dissolution of the Soviet Union and his resignation as president.
* The decline of communism meant that the Soviet Union had much less influence on other countries. This had already resulted in the end of the Warsaw Pact in July 1991.

Propaganda – It was hard for the Soviet Union to 'sell' communism when capitalism seemed to work better and give people more.

Afghan War – The huge cost of this long war was a major drain on the Soviet Union's economy.

Economy – The Soviet economy was never as productive as that of the USA.

Why did the Soviet Union lose the Cold War?

Arms race – Catching up with the USA in the 1960s crippled the Soviet economy.

Freedom – The Eastern bloc and Soviet republics only existed because of force and repression.

1970s–80s – The Soviet Union's economy stagnated under Brezhnev while the USA forged ahead: for example while US firms developed personal computers, the Soviet Union feared what Soviet people might do with their own computers: print and distribute anti-Soviet documents?

Now try this

1 Explain how the Soviet Union collapsed between 1990 and 1991.
2 Give **three** reasons to explain the end of the Cold War.

Had a look ☐   Nearly there ☐   Nailed it! ☐

The significance of the fall of the Soviet Union

The collapse of the Soviet Union brought the Cold War to an end and resulted in the Soviet Union being divided up into different states.

The Soviet Union before its collapse in 1991

The Soviet Union before 1991.

After the collapse of the Soviet Union

After 1991 the Soviet Union fragmented into a range of different states in Europe and Asia, including Ukraine, the Baltic states and Kazakhstan.

The significance of the fall of the Soviet Union

- The Soviet Union became the Commonwealth of Independent States in January 1992.
- Many Soviet states seceded (broke away) from the Soviet Union and became independent states. These included Ukraine, Estonia, Latvia and Lithuania, as well as Asian Republics, such as Kazakhstan.

- The Cold War came to an end as the Soviet Union no longer existed and there was no ideological conflict between East and West. The meeting of Bush and Gorbachev in December 1989 (the Malta Summit) had already declared an end to the Cold War. This paved the way for the collapse of the Warsaw Pact, which was formally dissolved in July 1991.

Now try this

Explain **two** consequences of the fall of the Soviet Union.

Exam overview

This page introduces you to the main features and requirements of the
Paper 2 Option P4 exam paper.

About Paper 2

- Paper 2 is for both your period study and
  your British depth study.

- Superpower relations and the Cold War,
  1941–91 is a period study.

- Superpower relations and the Cold War is
  Option P4. You will see where it starts on
  the exam paper with a heading like this:

> The Paper 2 exam lasts for 1 hour 45
> minutes (105 minutes) in total. There are
> 32 marks for this period study and
> 32 marks for the British depth study, so
> you should spend about 50 minutes on each.

> Option P4: Superpower relations and the Cold War, 1941–91

- You will answer all the questions in
  this option. In question 3 you pick two
  statements to explain, out of a choice
  of three.

> Remember to read each question carefully
> before you start to answer it.

The three questions

The three questions for Superpower relations
and the Cold War will always follow this pattern.

Question 1

Explain **two** consequences of...   **(8 marks)**

> Question 1 focuses on consequences – things
> that happened as a result of something.

> There are four marks for Assessment
> Objective 1 (AO1). This is where you show
> your knowledge and understanding of the
> key features and characteristics.

> There are four marks for Assessment
> Objective 2 (AO2). This is where you explain and
> analyse key events using historical concepts:
> consequence in this case.

Question 2

Write a narrative account analysing...   **(8 marks)**

Two prompts and your own information

> Question 2 also targets both AO1
> and AO2. It asks you to provide an
> analytical narrative – an analysis of causation,
> consequence or change.

> Question 3 targets both AO1 and AO2
> and asks you to provide an analysis of
> consequence and significance – how important.

Question 3

Explain **two** of the following...   **(16 marks)**

Three statements each starting:

The importance of... for...

> You can see examples of all three questions
> on pages 32–40 of this Skills section, and
> in the practice section on pages 41–50.

Question 1: Explaining consequences 1

Question 1 on your exam paper will ask you to 'explain two consequences of...'.
There are 8 marks available for this question.

> ## Explaining consequences
>
> Consequences = results of. For consequences, think: 'what happened as a result of...?'
> To **explain** the consequences of an event, you need to:
>
> ☑ include **detail**, using your knowledge of the event
>
> ☑ **link** each consequence to the event that led to it.

Worked example

Explain **two** consequences of the Prague
Spring (1968).   **(8 marks)**

This question asks you to explain **two** results of the Prague Spring – that is, what the Prague Spring led to and **not** its causes.

 Links You can revise the Prague Spring on pages 13 and 16.

Sample answer

Consequence 1:

The Prague Spring led to greater freedoms in Czechoslovakia, or 'socialism with a human face'.

This is a correct consequence but the student has only given an outline answer. Make sure your answer **explains** the consequence.

Consequence 2:

The Prague Spring led to the Soviet invasion of Czechoslovakia in August 1968.

This is also a correct consequence and the beginning of an explanation. To improve this answer you would need to add more **detail** to the explanation.

Improved answer

Consequence 1:

The Prague Spring led to greater freedoms in Czechoslovakia, or 'socialism with a human face.' This resulted in a relaxation of press censorship, the legalisation of political opposition groups, toleration of political criticism and more powers being given to the Czechoslovakian parliament. It also led to market socialism, with the reintroduction of capitalist elements into the Czechoslovakian economy.

Remember to support your answer with detailed information about the topic.

Note how this answer shows a good understanding of the historical context and explains how the Prague Spring led to greater freedoms in Czechoslovakia.

Consequence 2:

The Prague Spring led to the Soviet invasion of Czechoslovakia in August 1968. Brezhnev was worried about the Prague Spring, as he felt that Dubček's reforms would be copied elsewhere in the Eastern bloc, undermining communism. Soviet media therefore began to portray Czechoslovakia as a massive threat to the Soviet Union, and in August 1968 Soviet and other Warsaw Pact troops invaded the country.

You can demonstrate good understanding of the **historical context** by showing how the Prague Spring led to Brezhnev eventually ordering the invasion of Czechoslovakia.

Be careful to support your explanation with detailed information about the topic.

Question 1: Explaining consequences 2

Question 1 is about explaining consequences and is worth 8 marks.

See pages 32 and 34 for more advice on answering Question 1.

Worked example

Explain **two** consequences of the Berlin Blockade (1948–49).   **(8 marks)**

This question asks you to explain **two** results of the Berlin Blockade, i.e. what the Berlin Blockade led to and **not** its causes.

 Links   You can revise the Berlin Blockade on page 7.

Sample answer

Consequence 1:

One consequence of the Berlin Blockade was that it led to the Berlin Airlift, when the British and Americans flew supplies into Berlin.

This is a correct consequence but here the student gives a vague answer. Make sure your answer explains the consequence.

Consequence 2:

Another consequence of the Berlin Blockade was that it led to the formation of the North Atlantic Treaty Organisation (NATO) – an alliance involving the United States and Western European countries.

This is also a correct consequence and the beginning of an explanation. To improve this answer you would need to add more to the explanation.

Improved answer

Support your explanation with detailed information about the topic.

Consequence 1:

The Berlin Blockade led to the Berlin Airlift. The Berlin Airlift involved British and American planes flying more than 1000 tonnes of supplies each day into West Berlin between June 1948 and May 1949. In January 1949 alone, more than 170 000 tonnes were flown in. This prevented the Berlin Blockade from succeeding, as supplies could still be delivered in spite of all road, rail and canal links to West Berlin being cut off. Moreover, Stalin could not shoot down the aircraft as this would have led to a full-scale war. In May 1949 Stalin called off the blockade.

This shows a good understanding of the historical context and how the problem of the Berlin Blockade was solved by the Berlin Airlift.

Link the Berlin Airlift with the Berlin Blockade, to show how the blockade led directly to the airlift.

Consequence 2:

The formation of NATO was also a consequence of the Berlin Blockade. Fears that Stalin's aggression over Berlin would be repeated led to other European Countries forming the North Atlantic Treaty Organisation. These included Norway, France, Belgium, Holland, Britain, Italy and the United States. This alliance was based around the principle of collective security where if one country came under (communist) attack then all others would come to its assistance.

Note how this answer shows a good understanding of the historical context.

By linking the consequence to the Berlin Blockade, you will show how the Berlin Blockade led directly to the establishment of NATO.

Remember to support your explanation with detailed information about the topic.

Question 1: Explaining consequences 3

Question 1 is about explaining consequences and is worth 8 marks.

See pages 32 and 33 for more advice on answering Question 1.

Worked example

Explain **two** consequences of the break-up of the Eastern bloc (1989). **(8 marks)**

This question asks you to explain **two** results of the break up of the Eastern bloc – that is, what the break up of the Eastern bloc **led to** and not its causes.

Sample answer

Consequence 1:

The break up of the Eastern bloc led to the end of communism in many Eastern European states.

Consequence 2:

The break up of the Eastern bloc led to the end of the Warsaw Pact in July 1991.

 Links You can revise the break up of Eastern bloc on page 27.

This is a correct consequence, but the student has only given an outline answer. Make sure your answer **explains** the consequence.

This is also a correct consequence and the beginning of an explanation. To improve this answer you would need to add more **detail** to the explanation.

Improved answer

Consequence 1:

One consequence of the break up of the Eastern bloc was the end of communism in Eastern European states. In December 1988, Gorbachev had stated that ideology would play a smaller part in foreign affairs. This encouraged East European states to hold free elections. These included Poland (June 1989), Hungary (summer 1989) and Czechoslovakia (November 1989); each resulted in the election of non-communist governments. By the end of 1990, no East European country had a communist government.

Consequence 2:

Another consequence of the break up of the Eastern bloc was the end of the Warsaw Pact in July 1991. The emergence of non-communist governments in Eastern Europe meant there was no longer a reason for the Warsaw Pact, an alliance of communist states, to exist. So the Warsaw Pact was dissolved following a meeting of East European leaders in Hungary, on 25 February 1991. The Warsaw Pact formally ended in July 1991.

Do refer to the word 'consequence' in your answer – it shows the examiner that you are answering the question.

Support your answer with **detailed information** about the topic.

Notice how this answer shows good understanding of the **historical context** and explains how the break-up of the Eastern bloc led to the end of communism in Eastern Europe.

You can demonstrate good understanding of the historical context by explaining how the collapse of the Eastern bloc led to the end of the Warsaw Pact.

Remember to support your answer with detailed information about the topic.

Question 2: Writing analytical narrative 1

Question 2 on your exam paper will ask you to 'write a narrative account analysing...'. There are 8 marks available for this question. A narrative account explains how events led to an outcome.

See pages 36 and 37 for more advice on answering Question 2.

Worked example

Write a narrative account analysing the key events of the crisis over Berlin in the years 1958–61.

You may use the following in your answer:

- the refugee crisis
- the construction of the Berlin Wall.

You **must** also use information of your own.

(8 marks)

Sample answer

The crisis over Berlin in the years 1958–61 occurred because of the refugee crisis that existed in East Germany. Between 1949 and 1961, about 2.7 million people migrated from East Germany to West Berlin and then to West Germany. This was a problem for Khrushchev, as it implied that East Germans preferred capitalism to communism; this was a propaganda disaster for him. It also created a skills shortage in East Germany, as many of those who migrated did so because wages were higher in West Germany than in East Germany.

As a result, Khrushchev issued an ultimatum in November 1958 demanding that the Western powers remove their troops from Berlin. However, Khrushchev could not risk a war with the United States, which could escalate into a nuclear confrontation.

To try and avoid this, Khrushchev and the Americans organised a series of summit meetings at Geneva (May 1959), Camp David (September 1959), Paris (May 1960) and Vienna (June 1961). None of these summits succeeded and by 1961 there was a real risk of war between the US and the Soviet Union, as well as a series of military alerts in Berlin.

Khrushchev responded by building the Berlin Wall in August 1961. This kept East Berliners in East Berlin and prevented any more from 'escaping' to the West. In future, any East Germans attempting to cross into West Germany would be shot.

Explaining connections

For this question, you need to consider how key events were **connected**. As with all the questions on this paper, you need to think about **consequences** and **causes**: what happened as a result of a key event.

Information of your own

The question states that 'you **must** also use information of your own'. Make sure you do this. In this answer, the student includes their own information about the Berlin ultimatum and the summit meetings from 1959–1961.

Logical structure

If you plan your answer by noting down your key events first on scrap paper, this will help you structure your answer into a clear and logical sequence. Start with the earliest key event and work from one event to the next, identifying consequences, causes and changes.

Chronology

Make sure you get the chronology right. This will enhance the quality of your answer. Drawing a brief timeline before you answer the question may help here.

 Links You can revise this topic on pages 11 and 14.

Links

Once you have identified the key events, your answer should consider how one key event links to the next. This answer has signposted this with phrases such as 'as a result'.

Question 2: Writing analytical narrative 2

Question 2 is about writing analytical narrative and is worth 8 marks.

See pages 35 and 37 for more advice on answering Question 2.

Worked example

Write a narrative account analysing how the 'Second Cold War' developed between 1979 and 1985.

You may use the following in your answer:

- the Soviet invasion of Afghanistan (1979)
- the Strategic Defence Initiative (SDI).

You **must** also use information of your own.

(8 marks).

Sample answer

The Soviet invasion of Afghanistan led to the removal of President Amin from power and his replacement by Barbrak Karmal. Soviet troops were required to remain in Afghanistan to keep Karmal in power. Brezhnev had mistakenly believed that President Carter would interpret the invasion as the Soviet Union reasserting control over its own sphere of influence in Afghanistan, a country on its own borders.

As a result, relations got worse as Carter felt that the invasion threatened US interests in the Middle East. This resulted in the Carter Doctrine, which said the USA would challenge any threat to US interests in the Middle East.

This meant that relations got even worse as the USA now aided the Afghan rebels, the Mujahideen, who were fighting Soviet troops. The US also imposed economic sanctions (a grain embargo) on the Soviet Union and boycotted the Moscow Olympics in 1980. The Soviet Union responded by boycotting the Los Angeles Olympics in 1984.

Moreover, the Soviet invasion of Afghanistan also strengthened fears of communism in the USA and led to the election of President Reagan, a staunch anti-communist who described the Soviet Union as the 'Evil Empire'. Reagan began to increase US defence expenditure and in 1983 announced the development of the Strategic Defence Initiative (Star Wars); a system of mirrors and lasers in space designed to shoot down incoming missiles

Analytical narrative

✓ Organise your answer using sufficient detail to answer the question.

✓ **Link** the events together to create a coherent narrative.

✓ Use your own information. This is very important for the best answers – don't just rely on the bullet points in the question!

 You can revise this topic on pages 24–26.

Remember to pick out the key events and link them together. The key events in this question are the Soviet invasion of Afghanistan, the Carter Doctrine, the non-ratification of SALT 2, the election of Ronald Reagan and SDI.

Information of your own

Remember the question states that 'you must also use information of your own'. Make sure you do this. In this answer, the student includes their own information about the election of Reagan and the Carter Doctrine.

Structure and chronology

If you plan your answer by noting down your key events first on scrap paper, this will help you structure your answer into a clear and logical sequence. This can be done using a timeline, spider diagram or a mind map.

Key words

Key words and concepts such as 'Mujahideen', 'anti-communist' and 'boycotting' will improve the quality of your answer.

Links

You should consider how one key event links to the next. This answer has signposted this with phrases such as 'As a result relations got worse' and 'This meant that relations got even worse'.

Question 2: Writing analytical narrative 3

Question 2 is about writing analytical narrative and is worth 8 marks.

See pages 35 and 36 for more advice on answering Question 2.

Worked example

Write a narrative account analysing how relations between the United States and the Soviet Union improved between 1985 and 1987.

You may use the following in your answer:

- glasnost and perestroika
- the INF Treaty.

You **must** also use information of your own.

(8 marks).

Remember to **develop and explain the key points** in the question. Key points in this question include glasnost, perestroika, the summits between Reagan and Gorbachev, and the end of the New Cold War.

Sample answer

When Mikhail Gorbachev became leader of the Soviet Union he announced two new policies: **glasnost** (openness – making Soviet leaders more responsible for their actions) and **perestroika** (restructuring the way the Soviet Union was run). These policies meant that Gorbachev intended to improve communist rule in the Soviet Union. This meant that Gorbachev had to find a way of reducing the Soviet Union's defence expenditure, as it could not keep up with the United States' military spending. As a result, he entered into dialogue with President Reagan, who liked Gorbachev and believed he was sincere about reducing Cold War tensions.

This resulted in a series of summits, at Geneva (December 1985), Reykjavik (October 1986) and Washington (December 1987), where arms control was discussed. The conferences took place in a friendly manner, allowing differences over key issues, such as nuclear weapons, to be resolved. This resulted in the Intermediate-Range Nuclear Forces (INF) Treaty in December 1987, which eliminated all intermediate and short-range nuclear weapons in Europe (those with a range of 500 to 5500 kilometres).

 Links You can revise this topic on pages 22 and 23.

Information of your own

Remember the question states that you may use the two prompts it provides (the two bullet points) but also that 'you **must** also use information of your own'. Make sure you do use your own information as the best answers do this. In this answer, the student has included their own information about summits between Reagan and Gorbachev.

Logical structure and chronology

If you plan your answer by noting down the key events first on scrap paper, this will help you structure your answer into a clear and logical sequence. A brief timeline putting all the events in the right order will help you answer this question properly. Make sure you know the order in which key events occur.

Links

Once you have identified the key events, your answer should consider how one key event links to the next. This answer has signposted this with phrases such as 'This resulted in a series of summits' and 'This meant that Gorbachev had to find a way'.

Detail

Adding detail to your answer will improve the quality of your response.

Question 3: Explaining importance 1

Question 3 on your exam paper will ask you to explain the importance of something, for example, an event, a person or a development. You will be given a choice of three things to explain; you must answer two of them. There are 8 marks available for each answer, so Question 3 is worth 16 marks in total.

See pages 39 and 40 for more advice on answering Question 3.

Worked example

Explain **two** of the following:

- The importance of the SALT 1 Treaty (1972) for the development of the Cold War. **(8 marks)**

- The importance of the Soviet invasion of Afghanistan (1979) for relations between the US and the Soviet Union. **(8 marks)**

- The importance of the fall of the Berlin Wall (1989) for the development of the Cold War. **(8 marks)**

Choosing which point to answer

Although three bullet points are listed, the question only asks you to pick two of them for your answer: you should pick the two you can answer best and write two separate answers for this question.

This student answer **below** is about the fall of the Berlin Wall.

Sample answer

The fall of the Berlin Wall (1989) was important because it confirmed the collapse of communism in Eastern Europe. The fall of the Berlin Wall unified Germany. It ended communist rule in East Germany and other communist countries in Eastern Europe.

In 1968 Brezhnev, via the Brezhnev Doctrine, established that the Soviet Union had the right to intervene in states that threatened to leave the Warsaw Pact. Gorbachev's unwillingness to do so in the case of East Germany meant that the Warsaw Pact collapsed, as many countries, such as Hungary and Poland, left the alliance, which was formally dissolved in July 1991.

This in turn meant that the fall of the Berlin Wall was important in helping the Cold War in Europe come to an end. The Berlin Wall's collapse led to the end of the Iron Curtain, as Germans could travel between East and West Germany. Europe was no longer divided between communist Eastern Europe and capitalist Western Europe. This was confirmed at the Malta Summit (1989), where Bush and Gorbachev formally announced the end of the Cold War.

Remember: do **not** describe what happened. Explain **why** it was important.

Links

Your answer should consider how one key event links to the next. This answer has signposted this with phrases such as 'led to' and 'this in turn meant that'.

Own knowledge

Make sure you use your own detailed knowledge. In this answer the student has included information about the Brezhnev Doctrine.

Logical structure

If you plan your answer by noting down your key events first on scrap paper, this will help you structure your answer into a clear and logical sequence.

Consequence

You need to understand and **learn** the chronology – the order in which events occur – to do well in questions such as this. Thus, the fall of the Berlin Wall was followed by the unification of Germany (1990) and the collapse of the Warsaw Pact (July 1991).

 Links You can revise the fall of the Berlin Wall on page 28.

Question 3: Explaining importance 2

Question 3 is about explaining importance and is worth 16 marks. You will be given a choice of three things to explain; you must answer **two** of them.

See pages 38 and 40 for more advice on answering Question 3.

Worked example

Explain **two** of the following:

- The importance of the SALT 1 Treaty (1972) for the development of the Cold War. **(8 marks)**
- The importance of the Soviet invasion of Afghanistan (1979) for relations between the USA and the Soviet Union. **(8 marks)**
- The importance of the fall of the Berlin Wall (1989) for the development of the Cold War. **(8 marks)**

 Links You can revise the Soviet invasion of Afghanistan on pages 24 and 25.

Importance and significance

Question 3 tests your ability to explain how and why an event is significant. A strong answer would explain two or three consequences of the event and contain relevant factual knowledge. The best answers will also be organised and flow smoothly, something you can achieve by using 'linking' phrases such as 'It was also important because it led to...' or 'Thirdly, it meant that...'

Sample answer

The Soviet invasion of Afghanistan was important because it led to the Carter Doctrine and brought an end to détente.

For President Carter, the Soviet invasion of Afghanistan led to a threat to US interests in the Middle East, especially its oil supply. To protect these interests, Carter announced the Carter Doctrine, which asserted that the USA would take steps to protect its interests in the Middle East. This meant that if the Soviet Union threatened the Middle East and its oil supplies the United States would respond.

This in turn led to the collapse of détente as the United States no longer trusted the Soviet Union. The US Senate never ratified SALT 2 and Carter also announced that the United States would be boycotting the Moscow Olympics (1980). Finally, Carter introduced a grain embargo against the Soviet Union.

The invasion of Afghanistan, by heightening fears of communism, also led to the election of Ronald Reagan as president. This led to the 'Second Cold War' (1981–85), as relations declined further.

This student answer is about the Soviet invasion of Afghanistan.

Links

Your answer should consider how one key event links to the next. This answer has signposted this with phrases such as 'led to' and 'this meant that'.

Own knowledge

Make sure you use your own detailed knowledge; the best answers do this. In this answer the student has included information about the Carter Doctrine.

Logical structure

If you plan your answer by noting down your key events first on scrap paper, this will help you structure your answer into a clear and logical sequence.

Addressing the question

Make sure you show how your event affected the way in which the USA and the Soviet Union viewed and dealt with each other. Did relations get worse or better as a result of the invasion?

Question 3: Explaining importance 3

Question 3 is about explaining importance and is worth 16 marks. You will be given a choice of three things to explain; you must answer **two** of them.

See pages 38 and 39 for more advice on answering Question 3.

Worked example

Explain **two** of the following:
- The importance of the SALT 1 Treaty (1972) for the development of the Cold War. **(8 marks)**
- The importance of the Soviet invasion of Afghanistan (1979) for relations between the USA and the Soviet Union. **(8 marks)**
- The importance of the fall of the Berlin Wall (1989) for the development of the Cold War. **(8 marks)**

Sample answer

The Strategic Arms Limitation Treaty (SALT 1) was important because it strengthened détente and led to further arms control negotiations.

SALT 1 limited the number of missiles and bombers available to each side, so was important because it increased trust between the USA and the Soviet Union. This strengthened détente, resulting in trade agreements between the USA and the Soviet Union where the Soviet Union exported oil to the United States and the Soviet Union received surplus US grain. It also led to the Helsinki Treaty (1975) and further cooperation in space (the Apollo Soyuz mission) in 1975.

SALT 1 was also important because it led to further arms control negotiations resulting in the SALT 2 agreement in June 1979 although this was never ratified by the US Senate.

 Links You can revise the SALT 1 Treaty on page 20.

Logical structure

If you plan your answer by noting down your key events first on scrap paper, this will help you structure your answer into a clear and logical sequence.

Explaining importance

To explain importance you need to use your own knowledge and understanding of the period to talk about the consequences and significance of an event, a person or a development. Think about what difference the event, person or development made to what happened next.

Understanding the chronology

The word 'chronology' refers to the order in which events occur. Make sure that you learn and understand the chronology around your question. Drawing up a brief timeline before you answer the question will help you answer it more effectively.

The student answer opposite is about the SALT 1 Treaty.

Do **not** describe what happened. Explain **why** it was important.

Signposting

Note how the opening paragraph identifies or 'signposts' the points that are developed later. This makes the response easier to write and mark. Using the word 'important' tells the examiner that you are answering the question.

Links

Your answer should consider how one event contributed to another. This answer has signposted this with phrases such as 'led to' and 'this resulted in'.

Own knowledge

Make sure you use your own detailed knowledge as the best answers do this. In this answer, the student has included information about SALT 1 and SALT 2.

Practice

Put your skills and knowledge into practice with the following question.

> **Option P4: Superpower relations and the Cold War, 1941–91**
>
> Answer ALL questions in this section.
>
> **1.** Explain **two** consequences of the crisis in Berlin in 1958–61.
>
> **(8 marks)**
>
> **Consequence 1:**
>
> **Guided**   One consequence of the Berlin crisis was that
>
> it led to the construction of the Berlin Wall
>
> ....
>
> ....
>
> ....
>
> ....
>
> ....
>
> ....
>
> ....
>
> ....
>
> ....
>
> ....
>
> **Consequence 2:**
>
> ....
>
> ....
>
> ....
>
> ....
>
> ....
>
> ....
>
> ....
>
> ....
>
> ....
>
> ....
>
> ....

You have 1 hour 45 minutes for the **whole** of Paper 2, so you should spend about **50 minutes** on this option. Remember to leave 5 minutes or so to check your work when you've finished writing.

 Links You can revise the Berlin crisis on pages 7 and 14

The word 'explain' requires you to make clear with sufficient detail how the Berlin crisis led to the consequences you have chosen. Use phrases such as 'led to' or 'resulted in' here.

A **consequence** is something that happens after an earlier event, so this question is asking you to name and explain two things that happened as a result of the Berlin crisis.

Make sure you explain how the Berlin crisis led to the consequence you have chosen, and remember to support your answer with sufficient detail.

Your exam paper will have a separate space for each feature you need to describe.

Practice

Put your skills and knowledge into practice with the following question.

2. Write a narrative account analysing the key events of the Soviet invasion of Afghanistan and how the Americans reacted to it (1979-80).

You may use the following in your answer:

- Soviet concerns about Afghanistan
- the Carter Doctrine.

You **must** also use information of your own.　**(8 marks)**

Guided　The Soviet invasion of Afghanistan occurred

....

as a result of Soviet concerns about communist rule

....

in Afghanistan.

....

....

....

....

....

....

....

....

....

....

....

....

....

....

....

....

....

....

....

....

....

....

....

....

Links　You can revise the Soviet invasion of Afghanistan on pages 24 and 25.

Remember that Question 2 is all about narrative. This means you are required to produce a **structured account** explaining how an event happened.

There are 8 marks on offer for this question. You don't have to use the prompts in the question but you **must** include your own information to answer the question fully. However, any answer to this question should refer to the Mujahedeen and the Carter Doctrine. Reference to the Olympic boycotts and the non-ratification of the SALT 2 Treaty would also be useful.

Your narrative needs to stay focused on answering the question. You may remember lots of detail about the Soviet invasion of Afghanistan but you need to include this in a **structured account** that answers the question set. Try and write three to four paragraphs that do this.

Remember: the best answers to Question 2 will demonstrate good knowledge and **understanding** of the key features and characteristics of the Soviet invasion of Afghanistan and its consequences.

Practice

Use this page to continue your answer to Question 2.

....

....

.... ◀ You might mention the US reaction to the Soviet invasion of Afghanistan and the end of détente.

....

....

....

....

....

....

.... ◀ Remember: you are required to produce a **structured account** explaining how an event happened. Focus on the order of events and try to link them together.

....

....

....

....

.... ◀ You might mention the election of President Reagan and the New Cold War.

....

....

....

....

....

....

....

....

....

....

....

....

....

....

....

....

....

Practice

Put your skills and knowledge into practice with the following question.

3. Explain **two** of the following:

- The importance of the events in Cuba in 1962 for the development of the Cold War. **(8 marks)**
- The importance of the Marshall Plan (1947) for relations between the US and the Soviet Union. **(8 marks)**
- The importance of the break up of the Eastern bloc (1989) for relations between the United States and the Soviet Union. **(8 marks)**

(Total for Question 3 = 16 marks)

Remember: you only have to **explain two** out of the three events.

This page will come first, then the answer pages where you indicate your choices.

This question asks you to look at why an event is important or significant. You must refer, therefore, to its **consequences** – what it led to or contributed towards.

  Links You can revise events in Cuba on pages 12 and 15. For more about the Marshall Plan, turn to pages 5 and 6. Find out more about the break up of the Eastern bloc on pages 27–30.

If you decide to answer Question 3 (i), turn to page 45. If you decide to answer Question 3 (ii), turn to page 47. To answer Question 3 (iii), turn to page 49. can see examples of all three questions on pages 32–40 of this Skills section, and in the practice section on pages 41–50.

Avoid a descriptive approach. Instead think of at least two important consequences of the event mentioned in the question.

Write a sentence defining your event and then at least two paragraphs explaining its importance. Remember to include sufficient detail in your answer and try to link your consequences together.

Answering the question

On the exam paper you will see exam question 3 on one page and then you'll turn onto a new page to start your answer to your first choice of question.

In the exam you will have two full pages of paper for each of the two questions that you choose to do.

You should spend about 12 minutes answering each of the questions you have chosen.

Practice

Put your skills and knowledge into practice with the following question.

Indicate which part you are answering by marking a cross in the box ☒. If you change your mind, put a line through the box ☒ and then indicate your new answer with a cross ☒.

☒ The importance of the events in Cuba in 1962 for the development of the Cold War.

☐ The importance of the Marshall Plan (1947) for relations between the US and the Soviet Union.

☐ The importance of the break up of the Eastern bloc (1989) for relations between the United States and the Soviet Union.

Guided   The Cuban Missile Crisis was important because it

almost resulted in a nuclear war.

....

....

....

....

....

....

....

....

....

....

....

....

....

....

....

....

....

....

....

....

....

Make sure you specify which question you are answering by putting a cross in the box.

Remember: you only have to **explain two** out of the three events.

🔗 **Links**   You can revise the events in Cuba by turning to pages 12 and 15.

Remember that you are looking at the consequences of the Cuban Missile Crisis. So plan your answer focusing on things such as:

Consequence	Led to
Brought the world to the brink of nuclear war.	Superpowers had to find ways of defusing future crises; Hotline Agreement, Partial Test Ban Treaty.
Khrushchev appeared to 'lose' the crisis as he agreed not to deploy the missiles in Cuba.	Khrushchev's fall from power (October 1964).

Remember: you are also looking at how significant the Cuban Missile Crisis was in the development of the Cold War. Did it increase or reduce Cold War tensions?

For each point you make, always then explain how it relates to the question.

Practice

Use this space to continue your answer to Question 3 (i) if necessary.

....

....

....

....

....

....

....

....

....

....

....

....

....

....

....

....

....

....

....

....

....

....

....

....

....

....

....

....

....

....

....

....

....

....

....

Remember: you need to write about the importance of the Cuban Missile Crisis. Don't just describe what happened.

You don't have to write a formal conclusion, but a single sentence summarising or briefly explaining your key points might help here. For example, you could say 'Overall the Cuban Missile Crisis was important because…', then add in your overall judgement. For instance, you might state that the Cuban Missile Crisis increased Cold War tensions in the short term but reduced them in the long term.

Make sure you support your explanation with a good range of accurate and relevant detail throughout your answer.

Practice

Put your skills and knowledge into practice with the following question.

Indicate which part you are answering by marking a cross in the box ☒. If you change your mind, put a line through the box ☒ and then indicate your new answer with a cross ☒.

☐ The importance of the events in Cuba in 1962 for the development of the Cold War.

☒ The importance of the Marshall Plan (1947) for relations between the USA and the Soviet Union.

☐ The importance of the break up of the Eastern bloc (1989) for relations between the United States and the Soviet Union.

Guided   The Marshall Plan was important because it led to about $13 billion of American money being given in financial aid to European countries.

....

....

....

....

....

....

....

....

....

....

....

....

....

....

....

....

....

....

....

....

....

Make sure you specify which question you are answering by putting a cross in the box.

Don't worry if you put a cross in the wrong box by mistake. Just put a line through the cross and then put a new cross in the right box.

Remember: you only have to **explain two** out of the three events.

Links   You can revise the importance of the Marshall Plan by turning to pages 5 and 6.

Remember that you are looking at the consequences of the Marshall Plan. So plan your answer focusing on things such as:

Consequence	Led to
Gave $13 billion of US money to Europe.	Improved the economies of many Western European countries. Communism seemed less attractive.
Some Eastern European countries, such as Czechoslovakia, also wanted the money.	This angered Stalin as it would undermine Soviet control in Eastern Europe.

Practice

Use this space to continue your answer to Question 3 (ii) if necessary.

Remember to keep writing about the importance of the Marshall Plan. Don't just describe what happened!

You don't have to write a formal conclusion, but a single sentence summarising or briefly explaining your key points might help here. For instance, you could say 'Overall, the Marshall Plan was important because it...' and then refer to how it angered the Soviet Union and contributed to the Berlin Blockade and the emergence of Comecon.

Practice

Put your skills and knowledge into practice with the following question.

Indicate which part you are answering by marking a cross in the box ☒. If you change your mind, put a line through the box ☒ and then indicate your new answer with a cross ☒.

☐ The importance of the events in Cuba in 1962 for the development of the Cold War.

☐ The importance of the Marshall Plan (1947) for relations between the USA and the Soviet Union.

☒ The importance of the break up of the Eastern bloc (1989) for relations between the United States and the Soviet Union.

Guided The collapse of the Eastern bloc was important

because it led to the cessation of communist rule

in Eastern Europe, the end of the Iron Curtain, the

reunification of Europe and the collapse of the Warsaw Pact.

....

....

....

....

....

....

....

....

....

....

....

....

....

....

....

....

....

....

....

You must put a cross in the box indicating the question you have chosen.

Remember: you only have to **explain two** out of the three events.

Plan your answer **before** you start writing. List the different ways in which the collapse of the Eastern bloc affected relations between the United States and the Soviet Union.

🔗 **Links** You can revise the importance of the break up of the Eastern bloc by turning to pages 27–30.

Remember: you are looking at the **consequences** of the break up of the Eastern bloc. So plan your answer focusing on things such as:

Consequence	Led to
The reunification of Europe and the collapse of the Iron Curtain.	Improved US – Soviet relations as Europe was no longer divided between communist/democratic governments.
Collapse of the Warsaw Pact (July 1991).	Improved US – Soviet relations as Europe no longer divided between competing alliance systems.

Practice

Use this space to continue your answer to Question 3 (iii) if necessary.

For each point you make, always then explain how it relates to the question.

Remember to keep writing about the importance of the break up of the Eastern bloc. Don't just describe what happened.

You don't have to write a formal conclusion, but a single sentence summarising or briefly explaining your key points might help here. For instance, you could say 'In overall terms the collapse of the Eastern bloc was important because...', then refer to the unification of Europe, the collapse of the Warsaw Pact, the Malta Summit and the end of the Cold War.

Answers

Where an example answer is given, this is not necessarily the only correct response. In most cases there is a range of responses that can gain full marks.

SUBJECT CONTENT

The origins of the Cold War, 1941–58
Early tension

1. The beginning of the Cold War

1 **Tehran Conference (1943):** USA and UK to open second front in Europe to take pressure off Soviet Union; Soviet Union to declare war on Japan once Germany was defeated; Poland to receive land from defeated Germany, but have some taken away by Soviet Union. Spheres of influence behind the discussions but not officially recorded: Eastern Europe for Soviet Union, Western Europe for UK, USA and France.

Yalta Conference (1945): Britain, the United States and the Soviet Union wanted Germany to be weakened once the war was over. This meant that they agreed that Germany was to be reduced in size, divided, demilitarised; to be democratic and to pay reparations when defeated; Nazi Party to be banned and war criminals tried. They also agreed that the United Nations would be set up to replace the League of Nations. They also agreed that the Soviet Union would declare war on Japan after the defeat of Germany and that the Soviet Union would have land Japan captured in earlier conflicts returned. However, they were forced to compromise over Poland: Britain and the United States wanted a democratic Poland; the Soviet Union wanted a country that was not hostile to it. This resulted in the decision that Poland should be in the Soviet sphere of influence but be 'democratic.'

Potsdam Conference (1945): At Potsdam the United States, the Soviet Union and Great Britain agreed that Europe should be rebuilt. This resulted in the setting up of a council of foreign ministers to organise the rebuilding of Europe. They also agreed that Germany would be weakened and placed under military occupation. This meant that the Nazi Party was to be banned; surviving Nazis were to be tried as war criminals in a special court run by the Allies at Nuremberg; Germany was to be reduced in size and divided into four zones, administered by the USA, the Soviet Union, Britain and France, with the aim of reuniting it under one government as soon as possible. Berlin was also divided up. The USA, Soviet Union and Great Britain also agreed that Germany had to pay reparations. This meant that each country was allowed to take reparations from the zone it occupied; the Soviet Union could have a quarter of the industrial equipment from the other three zones, because its zone was the least developed industrially, but had to provide the other zones with raw materials, such as coal.

2 November 1943 Tehran Conference, June 1944 D-Day landings (establishment of the Second Front), February 1945 Yalta Conference, May 1945 Germany surrenders, July 1945 Potsdam Conference.

2. The end of the Grand Alliance

1 Truman, Roosevelt's successor, was more suspicious of Stalin while Roosevelt wanted to work with him, Stalin disliked Truman personally and saw him as a threat to the Soviet Union, confirmed by the Novikov Telegram and the way that Truman tried to boss Stalin about at the Potsdam Conference.

2 Western leaders argued that communist democracy did not involve free and fair elections: voters could only vote for communist candidates – other parties were not allowed. Ordinary people, therefore, had no real choice over who governed them.

3. The breakdown of trust

1 The table you have created will help you compare and contrast, often opposing terms / issues. It is fairly easy to create one for capitalism vs. communism as they are complete opposites of each other!

2 (a) Communism's main criticism of capitalism was that it exploited the workers to make their bosses rich.

(b) Capitalism's criticism of communism was that it trampled on individual freedom and made everyone serve the state.

3 Trust between the United States and the Soviet Union declined because of the death of Roosevelt, ideological differences and growing mutual suspicion between the United States and the Soviet Union.

The death of Roosevelt was a key reason behind the collapse of relations between the United States and the Soviet Union. Roosevelt had been prepared to cooperate with Stalin at both the Tehran and Yalta conferences and believed that the Soviet Union, through the United Nations, could act as a diplomatic partner of the United States. Truman, however, was much more dismissive of the Soviet Union and believed that he could use the atomic bomb to bully the Soviet Union at the Potsdam Conference. This angered Stalin, thus straining the Soviet Union's relationship with the United States.

This tension was compounded by the ideological differences between the Soviet Union and the United States. The Soviet Union was a communist one-party state while the United States claimed to be a capitalist democracy. Communism had historically always been hostile to capitalism and sought to replace it, while in the 1920s the capitalist powers, including Britain and the United States, had tried to snuff out communism. Once their common enemy, Germany, had been defeated, both superpowers began to increasingly see each other as a threat.

This tension was further compounded by the growing mutual suspicion held between the USA and the Soviet Union. In the Long Telegram the US ambassador in Moscow argued that the Soviet Union was hostile to capitalism and was building up its military power. Similarly, in the Novikov telegram the Soviet ambassador in Washington argued that the United States wanted to dominate the world and was no longer interested in cooperation with the Soviet Union. This mutual suspicion meant that neither country trusted each other, causing relations to deteriorate.

4. Satellite states

Stalin gained control by establishing one-party states in Poland, Czechoslovakia, Hungary, Romania and Bulgaria using salami tactics. Stalin also set up bodies in the Eastern bloc, including Cominform and Comecon. Cominform allowed the Soviet Union to monitor the actions of East European governments, ensuring they remained loyal to the Soviet Union. Comecon, by forcing member states to trade with the Soviet Union, made sure they did not trade with the West and were under Soviet economic control.

The Cold War develops

5. The Truman Doctrine and the Marshall Plan

1 Any of the following are valid:

Western European countries experienced economic recovery, support for communism in Italy and France began to decline; the formation of NATO; Stalin was concerned that East European countries would accept Marshall Aid so undermining Soviet control in Eastern Europe; Marshall Aid benefitted West Germany; this worried Stalin and led to the Berlin Blockade.

2 The United States hoped that giving Marshall Aid would allow Western Europe's economies to recover. This would improve living standards and reduce support for Europe's communist parties.

6. Cominform, Comecon and NATO

Stalin was concerned that the Soviet Union's control in Eastern Europe would be weakened as countries turned to the United States rather than the Soviet Union. This would remove the Soviet Union's buffer zone, making it more vulnerable to attack from the West.

7. Germany and the Cold War

1 FRG = Federal Republic of Germany or West Germany; GDR = German Democratic Republic or East Germany; NATO = The North Atlantic Treaty Organisation

2 Stalin remained concerned about the reconstruction of the western zones of Germany. This resulted in a blockade, which began in June 1948. Stalin cut off all road, rail and canal links between Western Germany and West Berlin, with the aim of forcing the British, French and Americans to leave and uniting the city under communist control.

The Americans did not want to be forced to withdraw, as this would have been humiliating. Equally they did not want to provoke war by attempting to force supplies through to West Berlin. Instead they resorted to the Berlin Airlift, as this required the Soviets to shoot down US planes which, given the risk of a war between the USA and the Soviet Union, they were not prepared to do. As a result, 600–700 tonnes of supplies were airlifted into Berlin each day.

By May 1949 the Soviets found themselves unable to stop the blockade and lifted it, allowing supplies to resume by land to West Berlin. However, the crisis led to growing concerns over Soviet aggression in Europe, which in turn led to the establishment of NATO in 1949. Germany was also divided between East Germany (communist and loyal to the Soviet Union) and West Germany, which became democratic and part of NATO.

The Cold War intensifies

8. The arms race and the Warsaw Pact

The nuclear arms race was a significant development because it raised tensions between the superpowers. Both the United States and the Soviet Union feared that the other might gain a decisive advantage in nuclear weapons. This forced them in turn to spend more money on delivery systems (bombers and missiles) and warheads. By the mid-1950s both countries had developed thermonuclear weapons as well as missile systems. Both superpowers worried that new technology, including satellites, might give the other a decisive advantage and were suspicious of each other's intentions.

The arms race was also important because it affected the military strategy of both the United States and the Soviet Union. During the 1950s the Americans conceived of using nuclear weapons to counter the Soviet's numerically superior conventional forces. The Soviet Union also incorporated nuclear weapons into its military planning and increasingly used its nuclear arsenal to try and bully other states. For instance, in 1956, following the Hungarian and Suez crises, Khrushchev threatened to send rockets to London and Paris.

The Warsaw Pact was important because it created a command structure that gave the Soviet Union effective control of the armed forces of its East European satellite states. On paper at least, this increased the military power of the Soviet Union.

Equally importantly, the Warsaw Pact also mirrored NATO and resulted in Europe being divided up between two competing alliance systems. Both alliances therefore planned for the possibility of war with the other. This created a military balance in Europe.

9. Soviet control in Hungary

1 Many Hungarians were prepared to protest because they disliked communist rule. In particular, they disliked Hungary's dictator, Matyas Rakosi, known as the 'Bald Butcher'. Rakosi's repressive policies meant that by the early 1950s up to 5% of the population was imprisoned, including its religious leaders. Protests aimed to bring these policies to an end. Another reason was that food and consumer goods were transported to the Soviet Union, which reduced living standards. By protesting, Hungarians hoped to end these policies and improve their standard of living. Additionally, Khrushchev's secret speech, which denounced Stalin, persuaded many Hungarians that it was possible to protest against the regime without fear of arrest. Finally, the withdrawal of Soviet troops from Austria in 1954 may have persuaded some Hungarians that protest could result in a Soviet retreat from Hungary as well.

2 All of these things worried Khrushchev because he felt that if other East European countries did the same thing, then Soviet control over Eastern Europe and the Warsaw Pact would collapse. Khrushchev was also concerned about the violence of some of the protests. Attacks on party officials and secret policemen in Budapest and other towns and cities persuaded him that the authority of both the Hungarian Communist Party and the Soviet Union had been directly challenged.

10. The Soviet invasion of Hungary, 1956

1 Soviet concerns that Nagy threatened Soviet control over Hungary and Eastern Europe meant that he was executed and replaced by Janos Kadar, who pursued policies that the Soviet Union was prepared to tolerate. This meant Hungary remained a Soviet satellite state and a member of the Warsaw Pact. The violence of their invasion meant that Soviet actions were condemned internationally; however, the Suez Crisis in the Middle East provided a distraction and limited the damage to the Soviet Union's reputation, especially outside Europe.

2 Khrushchev remained concerned that events in Hungary could lead to the collapse of the Warsaw Pact. This resulted in Soviet military invasion, the arrest and execution of Nagy and his replacement by Kadar, who pursued policies that the Soviet Union was prepared to accept. This meant that Hungary remained in the Warsaw Pact.

Cold War crises, 1958–70
Increased tension
11. A divided Berlin

Any of the following reasons are valid:

1 West Berlin was an island of capitalism in East Germany; East Germans could escape to West Berlin, creating a refugee problem and skills shortage in East Germany; the Soviet Union wanted the Western powers to leave Berlin and this was something that the USA was not prepared to do; US and Soviet troops were close to each other in West Berlin, leading to the possibility of an incident happening.

2 Four summits occurred: in Geneva (May 1959), Washington (Sept 1959), Paris (May 1960) and Vienna (June 1961). None of the conferences reached agreement on the future of Berlin, leading to Khrushchev renewing his ultimatum that the West remove its troops from Berlin.

12. The Cuban Missile Crisis: origins

1 The Bay of Pigs incident occurred when Kennedy and the CIA tried to organise the overthrow of Castro by landing Cuban mercenaries (former supporters of Batista) on the northern coast of Cuba (at the Bay of Pigs – hence the name of the incident) with the aim of returning Batista to power. The invasion was easily defeated, strengthening Castro's grip on power in Cuba. Kennedy assumed that most Cubans would be anti-communist and would therefore support the invasion as a means of overthrowing Castro. The invasion failed because Batista had few supporters left in Cuba while the rebels lacked the military means to defeat Castro.

2 The invasion strengthened Castro's grip on power as ordinary Cubans clearly did not want Batista back. The invasion meant that Castro turned to the Soviet Union for support, receiving economic and military assistance. This increased Castro's dependence on the Soviet Union and meant that he accepted the deployment of Soviet missiles in Cuba. The Bay of Pigs was an embarrassment to Kennedy and the CIA and may have persuaded Khrushchev that Kennedy was a weak president.

3 The United States did not want a communist country close to its own borders. The Monroe Doctrine established that South America lay in a US sphere of influence just as Eastern Europe lay in the Soviet sphere of influence. The USA was therefore not prepared to accept countries like Cuba that challenged this.

13. Czechoslovakia and the Prague Spring

1 Dubček felt that communism needed to be genuinely popular in Czechoslovakia. To achieve this, he was prepared to give more power to regional governments, allow a relaxation of press censorship, tolerate the legalisation of opposition groups and criticism of the government as well as give more power to the Czechoslovakian parliament. He was also prepared to introduce 'market socialism' – the reintroduction of some capitalism into the Soviet economy.

2 People reacted to the Prague Spring in different ways because they had different perspectives on it. Younger Czechs and communists who had grown up

with harsh communist rule enthusiastically welcomed Dubček's reforms, as they felt they would encourage more freedoms, reduce oppression and boost living standards. Older communists, in Czechoslovakia, Eastern Europe and the Soviet Union, were horrified, as they felt that Dubček's reforms threatened communist rule across Eastern Europe and could result in the collapse of the Warsaw Pact.

Cold War crises

14. The construction of the Berlin Wall

1 Answers should refer to: the refugee problem in Berlin; US–Soviet summits did not resolve this problem and Khrushchev renewed his ultimatum that the West remove its troops from Berlin; the Berlin Wall was constructed (August 1961) to solve the refugee problem by preventing East Germans from entering West Berlin and avoiding war with the USA.

2 Khrushchev built the Berlin Wall to resolve the Berlin crisis and end the refugee problem in Berlin.

The refugee problem meant that thousands of East Germans were going to West Berlin and from there to West Germany. This created a skills shortage in East Germany. It was also humiliating for Khrushchev, because it seemed to demonstrate that ordinary people preferred capitalism to communism. This resulted in Khrushchev's ultimatum that British, French and American forces leave Berlin and that Berlin should be reunited under communist rule.

However, Khrushchev could not enforce this ultimatum, as it would result in war with the United States. For Khrushchev, building the wall would end the refugee crisis, as it would ensure that East Germans could no longer cross into West Berlin. At the same time it would also ensure that Berlin no longer had to be completely under Soviet control, reducing the risk of war with the United States.

15. The events of the Cuban Missile Crisis

Kennedy had a range of options: he could attack the sites (provoking a response from the Soviet Union and probably an attack on West Berlin); he could negotiate (this would lead to him being accused of weakness by his critics); or he could place an embargo on any imports (including missile parts) coming into Cuba. Kennedy chose the third option as it was now up to the Soviets to decide whether they wanted to break the embargo and provoke the United States.

This third option (the one that Kennedy actually chose) was perhaps the best one to recommend, as it forced the Soviet Union to back down without provoking a war with the United States. This was because it made the Soviets decide whether or not they wanted to risk war over deploying missiles in Cuba. Kennedy, therefore, could not be accused of deliberately trying to provoke

a war. It was also the least politically damaging: his political opponents in the United States would not accuse him of weakness, as he was standing up to the Soviet Union. The other option, attacking the sites, was dangerously reckless, as it would provoke a Soviet response, risking nuclear war.

16. The Brezhnev Doctrine and Soviet control in Czechoslovakia

1 May 1959 – Geneva Summit; September 1959 – Camp David Summit; May 1960 – Paris Summit; April 1961 – Bay of Pigs Incident; June 1961 – Vienna Conference; August 1961 – construction of the Berlin Wall; October 1962 – Cuban Missile Crisis; June 1963 – Hotline Agreement; August 1963 – Partial Test Ban Treaty; April 1968 – Prague Spring; August 1968 – Soviet invasion of Czechoslovakia. Nov 1968 – Khrushchev demands that Western forces withdraw from West Berlin.

2 Answers can mention: the Brezhnev Doctrine (this gave the Soviet Union the right to intervene in countries in Eastern Europe where communism was under threat); Czechoslovakia remained part of the Warsaw Pact; Romania and Yugoslavia condemned the attack and distanced themselves from the Soviet Union.

3 The Soviet invasion of Czechoslovakia was important to Soviet control of satellite states because it resulted in the Brezhnev Doctrine. This meant that the Soviet Union was prepared to invade countries that tried to reform communism. This discouraged other countries such as Poland from seeking to reform. This meant that Soviet-style communism continued even if people did not want it.

Reaction to crisis

17. The Berlin Wall and US–Soviet relations

1 Any of the following are valid: the Berlin Wall was a propaganda defeat for Khrushchev as it demonstrated that East Germans preferred life in West Germany and had to be imprisoned in East Germany; Berlin became a symbol of freedom, especially after Kennedy's visit in 1962; the Berlin Wall ended travel between East and West Berlin, cutting off many Germans from each other and dividing families; the Berlin Wall reduced the risk of a military confrontation between the Soviet Union and the United States.

2 Kennedy's speech was important because it was an expression of solidarity with West Berlin. His remark 'Ich bin ein Berliner' implied that the United States remained supportive of the existence and independence of West Berlin against Soviet aggression. This in turn strengthened NATO, as it implied the United States would also come to its assistance in the event of any future Soviet threat or ultimatum similar to that made by the Soviets over Berlin. The speech was also important as

West Berlin became a symbol of freedom in Soviet-dominated Eastern Europe, while the Berlin Wall, recently constructed by Khrushchev, symbolised oppression and tyranny. Kennedy's speech, delivered as it was not far from the Berlin Wall itself, therefore became a propaganda triumph for the United States.

18. The consequences of the Cuban Missile Crisis

1 The USA responded to the discovery of the missiles by setting up a quarantine zone around Cuba. This meant that any Soviet ships crossing the quarantine zone would be stopped, by force if necessary, creating the risk of an incident and the possibility of war. The USA also carried out aerial surveillance of Cuba, resulting in the shooting of a spy plane on 27 October. Both of these steps plus the possibility of a US invasion of Cuba resulted in a secret deal between the USA and the Soviet Union: the Soviet Union would withdraw its missiles from Cuba in return for American promises that there would be no invasion of Cuba and the secret removal of US missiles from Turkey.

2 Khrushchev's failure to deploy the missiles in Cuba meant that his authority was damaged within the Soviet Union and he was forced to resign in 1964. The crisis demonstrated the risks of nuclear war and Mutually Assured Destruction (MAD), leading to arms control agreements, such as the Hotline Agreement (1963), the Partial Test Ban Treaty (1963), the Outer Space Treaty (1967) and the Nuclear Non Proliferation Treaty (1969). These aimed to slow down the arms race and reduce the risk of nuclear war. It also weakened NATO, as France was no longer prepared to risk destruction in a nuclear war and left NATO's command structure in 1968.

19. International reaction to Soviet measures in Czechoslovakia

The Soviet invasion of Czechoslovakia provoked a negative response from Western European governments. The United States publically criticised the invasion, as did other Western governments including Britain and West Germany. However, the reaction was muted. The USA, already bogged down in the Vietnam War, made no attempt to come to Czechoslovakia's assistance. This made Brezhnev believe that any Soviet intervention in a country that was already communist would not be challenged by the United States. This view was proved disastrously wrong when the Soviets intervened in Afghanistan, then a communist country, in December 1979.

The invasion did, however, strengthen the Soviet grip on Eastern Europe. Under the Brezhnev Doctrine, the Soviet Union reserved the right to intervene militarily in instances where communist rule and the security of the whole Eastern bloc was threatened. This forced communist governments in Hungary and Poland to pursue policies acceptable to the Soviet Union or face Soviet invasion.

However, communist parties outside Eastern Europe, including those in Italy and France, condemned the attack. This was important because it reduced Soviet influence in Western Europe, as these parties began to pursue policies different to those of the Soviet Union.

The end of the Cold War, 1970–91 Attempts to reduce tension

20. Détente in the 1970s

1 Any two of the following: détente, by creating greater understanding between East and West, led to arms control agreements including the Strategic Arms Limitation Treaty (SALT 1), which placed limits on the number of bombers and missiles each side could possess. It also resulted in a greater cooperation in Europe and recognition of human rights, resulting in the Helsinki Agreements (1975). It also resulted in greater cooperation between the United States and the Soviet Union, including trade (the USA sold grain to the Soviet Union and imported Soviet oil) and in space (the Apollo Soyuz link up).

2 SALT 1 limited the number of nuclear weapons (SLBMs, bombers and ICBMs) available to each side. It slowed down the nuclear arms race and encouraged greater cooperation between the USA and the Soviet Union.

3 The Helsinki Agreements strengthened détente between the United States and the Soviet Union. This led to a stable relationship between the two countries. The Helsinki Agreements also stabilised the situation in Europe, as East and West Germany recognised each other's right to exist. It also led to greater economic cooperation between the USA and the Soviet Union: the USA bought oil from the Soviet Union and the Soviet Union bought wheat from the United States.

21. SALT 2 and the failure of détente

One key feature of SALT 2 was that it placed limits on the number of warheads used by both the United States and the Soviet Union. Both sides agreed to limit the number of warheads they possessed to 2250 each.

Another key feature of SALT 2 was that it was an agreement between the United States and the Soviet Union that did not involve the United States' allies, including West Germany. They worried that, as a result of the treaty, the United States would not be able to defend Europe from any future Soviet attack.

A final key feature of the SALT 2 treaty was that US Senate never ratified it, as a result of the Soviet invasion of Afghanistan in December 1979.

22. Changing attitudes

Relations between the United States and the Soviet Union gradually improved between 1985 and 1987. Gorbachev's ideas of glasnost and perestroika persuaded many Western leaders, including Thatcher and Reagan, that meaningful negotiations with the Soviet Union could take place. This led to three summit meetings: at Geneva (December 1985), Reykjavik (September 1986) and Washington (December 1987), resulting in the Intermediate-Range Nuclear Forces (INF) Treaty.

23. New thinking and the INF Treaty

The changing attitudes of Reagan and Gorbachev were important in improving superpower relations because Gorbachev, through his policies of glasnost and perestroika, wanted to reform the Soviet Union. This required reductions in defence spending, which in turn required arms control agreements and greater cooperation with the United States, thereby improving superpower relations. Reagan was also acutely aware of Gorbachev's popularity in Europe, known as 'Gorbymania'. This put pressure on him to soften his attitude towards the Soviet Union, which he had previously described as the 'evil empire', so improving relations between the two countries. Both countries were therefore happy to engage in summit diplomacy: they met in Geneva, Reykjavik and Washington, culminating in the Intermediate-Range Forces (INF) Treaty in December 1987.

Flashpoints
24. The significance of the Soviet invasion of Afghanistan

Answers should include reference to the following: Brezhnev saw Afghanistan as within the Soviet sphere of influence; the civil war of 1979, the overthrow and assassination of President Taraki and his replacement by Amin; Soviet mistrust of Amin leading to the Soviet invasion of December 1979 and his replacement by Barbrak Karmal.

25. The consequences of the Soviet invasion of Afghanistan

1   Any of the following points are valid: the invasion increased US mistrust of the Soviet Union and resulted in the end of détente. It also raised American fears about a Soviet threat to US oil supplies in the Middle East, resulting in the Carter Doctrine. It increased opposition to SALT 2 in the US Senate, which meant that the treaty was never ratified. The invasion resulted in a continuing Soviet military presence in Afghanistan, leading to attacks by the Mujahideen and rising Soviet casualties. The invasion also resulted in US support for the Mujahideen, increasing Cold War tensions further.

2   It ended détente, as both superpowers no longer trusted each other. 'Peaceful co-existence" between the Soviet Union and the United States thus came to an end. This led to the election of President Reagan as US president; he had a much more hostile attitude towards the Soviet Union, resulting in a ´Second Cold War` between the superpowers. The invasion also led to the Carter Doctrine, by which the USA was prepared to use force if the Soviet Union threatened its strategic interests in the Middle East (its oil supply). The invasion also led to the Olympic boycotts of 1980 (Moscow) and 1984 (Los Angeles), as well as US support for the Mujahideen in Afghanistan.

26. Reagan and the 'Second Cold War'

1   Relations between the United States and the Soviet Union declined in a number of ways: the arms race intensified (MX Missile, SDI); cooperation between the USA and the Soviet Union declined (Olympic boycotts in 1980 and 1984); the Reagan presidency ushered in a new era of Cold War activity; tension over the war in Afghanistan; the shooting down of KAL007.

2   Any of the following points are valid: SDI broke the terms of both SALT 1 and the Outer Space Treaty, which placed limits on missile defence systems and the deployment of weapons systems in space. SDI potentially gave the Americans a first strike capacity in any nuclear war and suggested that the USA was not interested in arms control, damaging further the relationship between the United States and the Soviet Union. SDI forced the Soviets to retaliate, thereby intensifying the arms race. The need to match SDI placed an intolerable burden on the Soviet economy, forcing Gorbachev to negotiate with the United States.

The collapse of Soviet control
27. The loosening Soviet grip on Eastern Europe

The loosening Soviet grip on Eastern Europe began with Gorbachev's succession as leader of the Soviet Union. In December 1988 he announced that ideology should play a smaller role in foreign affairs, which suggested that the Brezhnev Doctrine no longer applied. This meant that East European leaders were free to embark on reforms without worrying about Soviet military intervention, as happened in Hungary (1956) and Czechoslovakia (1968). This led to free elections in Poland (June 1989) and Hungary (Spring 1989), which led to the Communist Party being defeated there. This was followed by further change in Czechoslovakia (the Velvet Revolution), Bulgaria and East Germany (where the Berlin Wall fell, the East German Government collapsed and Germany was reunited under a democratically elected government). In all these cases, political change was peaceful. Only in Romania was violence required to secure political change, where force was required to overthrow the dictatorship of Ceausescu.

28. The fall of the Berlin Wall

1 Any two of the following points are valid: The fall of the Berlin Wall damaged the authority of the communist government and led to the collapse of communist rule in East Germany. It also encouraged protests elsewhere and resulted in the collapse of communist rule in other Eastern European countries, including Czechoslovakia (November 1989) and Romania and Bulgaria (December 1989). The emergence of non-communist governments resulted in the end of the Warsaw Pact in July 1991, as these governments no longer had any ideological reasons to continue this alliance. The end of the Warsaw Pact and communist rule in Eastern Europe also resulted in the collapse of the Iron Curtain and the reunification of Europe, as the communist half of Europe had disappeared by 1991. The collapse of the Wall also removed a major cause of conflict between East and West, so ending the Cold War. At the Malta Summit (December 1989) Bush and Gorbachev announced that the Cold War had come to an end.

2 The emergence of Gorbachev as leader of the Soviet Union led to the end of the Brezhnev Doctrine. In December 1988 Gorbachev announced that ideology would no longer play a role in Soviet foreign affairs. This was a clear signal that the Soviet Union would not intervene if these countries began to move away from Soviet-style communism. This resulted in Poland and Hungary embracing reform. Poland and Hungary held free elections in the summer of 1989. This, in turn, put pressure on more hardline communist governments in East Germany, Czechoslovakia, Romania and Hungary to grant similar reforms. This, combined with a lack of Soviet support, meant that even these governments found it hard to resist public pressure for reform. This resulted in the collapse of the Berlin Wall in November 1989 and the end of communist rule in East Germany. This then created a momentum that swept away communist rule in Czechoslovakia (The Velvet Revolution), Romania and Bulgaria. By early 1990 communist rule had collapsed across Eastern Europe. Europe was no longer divided between East and West bringing an end to the Iron Curtain.

29. The end of the Cold War

1 The collapse of the Soviet Union occurred because Gorbachev, in spite of his popularity abroad, could not improve the Soviet economy at home. This meant that many ordinary Russians now demanded further reforms, including the end of communist rule, while others in Estonia, Latvia, Lithuania and Ukraine demanded independence from the Soviet Union. The failure of the August Coup (August 1991) strengthened demand for reform, resulting in the resignation of Gorbachev and the dissolution of the Soviet Union.

2 The Cold War ended because of the policies of Gorbachev, the collapse of the Eastern Bloc and the fall of the Iron Curtain.

Gorbachev's policies of *glasnost* and *perestroika* meant that the Soviet Union needed to improve its economy and reduce its defence expenditure. This necessitated increased cooperation with the United States, resulting in summit diplomacy (Reagan and Gorbachev met at Geneva, Reykjavik and Washington) culminating in the INF Treaty being signed in December 1987 (which reduced the number of intermediate range nuclear weapons each side possessed). It also opened the door to further arms reductions agreements, culminating in the Conventional Forces in Europe (CFE) Treaty in 1990 and the Strategic Arms Reduction Treaty (START) in 1991.

Gorbachev's desire to improve relations with the United States also meant that he had to take a softer line in Eastern Europe. He therefore abandoned the Brezhnev Doctrine, claiming that ideology would play a smaller role in Soviet foreign affairs. This encouraged East European governments to begin democratic reforms. This led to the end of communist rule in Poland and Hungary, the fall of the Berlin Wall and the end of communist rule in East Germany. It also resulted in the collapse of communism in Czechoslovakia, Romania and Bulgaria. This led to the fall of the Iron Curtain and the unification of Europe. This was because Europe was no longer divided up between two competing alliances and different political systems – capitalism and communism. In December 1989 President Bush and Gorbachev, meeting at Malta, announced an official end to the Cold War, and in July 1991 the Warsaw Pact was dissolved.

30. The significance of the fall of the Soviet Union

Any of the following points are valid: the collapse of the Soviet Union resulted in the end of communist rule, as many of the new successor states embraced democracy resulting in the election of non-communist governments. The break up of the Soviet Union resulted in the formation of new independent states including Estonia, Latvia, Lithuania and Ukraine, as they no longer wanted Russia to govern them. It also resulted in the end of the Cold War, as there was no longer an ideological conflict between East and West.

PRACTICE
41. Practice

1 **Consequence 1:** One consequence of the Berlin crisis was that it led to the construction of the Berlin Wall. The East German government faced a crisis as skilled workers, many of whom already worked in West Berlin, crossed to West Berlin and then to West Germany. Between 1949 and 1961, 2.7 million East Germans were able to enter West Germany this way. This meant that by the early 1960s the East German government was facing a skills shortage, as doctors, engineers and other skilled workers left for the higher wages and

better quality of life found in the West. This resulted in the construction of the Berlin Wall in August 1961; a measure designed to keep East Germans in East Germany by preventing them from crossing to the West. In future anyone escaping East Germany by crossing the Wall would be shot.

Consequence 2: Another consequence of the Berlin crisis was that it led to an increase in tension between the superpowers. Khrushchev's ultimatum that British, French and American forces leave West Berlin led to an ongoing series of military alerts in the city. Further, the series of summits organised at Geneva, Camp David, Paris and Vienna could do little to resolve the problem, creating the possibility that the Soviet Union might use force to drive the West out of Berlin. Ironically it was the building of the Wall that reduced tension. As Kennedy stated, "It's not a very nice solution, but a wall is a hell of a lot better than a war."

42. Practice

2 The Soviet invasion of Afghanistan occurred as a result of Soviet concerns about communist rule in Afghanistan. In 1978 Afghanistan had become a Soviet ally and had promised to 'build socialism in Afghanistan'. However, following a civil war, Taraki was forced to share power with Hazifullah Amin, who, in October 1979, murdered Taraki and claimed the Presidency for himself. This prompted a Soviet invasion that resulted in Amin's death; his replacement with Barbrak Karmal. However, Soviet troops were required to stay in the country to keep Karmal in power. This resulted in a guerrilla war fought by the Mujahideen, aimed at driving the Soviets out and removing Karmal's government. Brezhnev had assumed that the Americans would ignore the invasion, just as they had done in respect of Czechoslovakia in 1968. However, President Carter was worried, as he saw the Soviet invasion as a threat to US interests in the Middle East, especially its oil supply. This led to the Carter Doctrine, which asserted that the Middle East was an area of special interest to the United States and that they would take steps to counter any Soviet threat there. This led to US support for the Mujahideen, trade sanctions against the Soviet Union and the American boycott of the Moscow Olympic Games (1980). Moreover, the US Senate failed to ratify the SALT 2 treaty while US defence spending increased by 5%. By 1980, therefore, détente was dead and a new era, the ´Second Cold War`, was beginning.

44. Practice

3 The importance of the events in Cuba in 1962 for the development of the Cold War.

The Cuban Missile Crisis was important because it almost resulted in a nuclear war. If Soviet ships had crossed the Quarantine Zone that the United States had placed around Cuba then an incident could have occurred which may have escalated into nuclear war. Similarly, the shooting down of a US spy plane over Cuba on 27 October 1962 could also have escalated dangerously. This resulted in attempts by the superpowers to ensure that future crises were properly managed and did not spin out of control. This led to the signing of the Hotline Agreement (1963), which set up a telephone line between Washington and Moscow, to be used in the event of future crises. The Cuban Missile Crisis was also important because it appeared to represent a failure for Khrushchev, as he had to agree not to deploy missiles in Cuba. This damaged his reputation within the Russian Communist Party and was one of the factors that led to his removal from office and replacement with Leonid Brezhnev in October 1964.

47. Practice

3 The importance of the Marshall Plan (1947) for relations between the USA and the Soviet Union.

The Marshall Plan was important because it led to about $13 billion of American money being given in financial aid to European countries. This improved living standards in a Europe still recovering from the Second World War, making communism less attractive to Western European voters. This was especially important in countries such as Italy and France, which had powerful communist parties. Marshall Aid was also important because it angered the Soviet Union. At the Paris Conference (1948), Soviet delegates stormed out claiming that Marshall Aid was the first step in creating a military alliance that would invade the Soviet Union. The Soviet Union was therefore very aggressive towards East European countries such as Czechoslovakia, which expressed interest in receiving Marshall Aid. In 1948 Czechoslovakia became a one-party state in common with all other East European countries. Similarly, the Soviet Union became increasingly concerned that western Germany was in receipt of Marshall Aid, something that led to Stalin's decision to launch the Berlin Blockade in June 1948.

49. Practice

3 The importance of the break up of the Eastern bloc (1989) for relations between the United States and the Soviet Union.

The break up of the Eastern bloc was important because it led to the fall of the Berlin Wall and the collapse of communist East Germany by 1990. This improved relations between the United States and the Soviet Union, because Berlin no longer remained a divisive issue between East and West. The break up of the Eastern bloc was also important because it led to the collapse of the Warsaw Pact. Military cooperation ceased in early 1990 and the Pact was formally dissolved in July 1991. This boosted relations between the USA and the Soviet Union, as Europe was no longer divided into two armed camps. This resulted in the START I Agreement (1991), which reduced missile stockpiles and made it easier to achieve a Conventional Forces in Europe (CFE) Agreement in 1990.

Notes

Notes

Notes

Published by Pearson Education Limited, 80 Strand, London, WC2R 0RL.

www.pearsonschoolsandfecolleges.co.uk

Copies of official specifications for all Pearson qualifications may be found on the website: qualifications.pearson.com

Text © Pearson Education Limited 2016
Produced, typeset and illustrated by Tech-set Ltd, Gateshead
Cover illustration by Kamae Design Ltd

The right of Brian Dowse to be identified as author of this work has been asserted by him in accordance with the Copyright, Designs and Patents Act 1988.

Content is included from Rob Bircher, Kirsty Taylor and Victoria Payne.

First published 2016

21
14

British Library Cataloguing in Publication Data
A catalogue record for this book is available from the British Library

ISBN 978 1 292 16975 0

Copyright notice
All rights reserved. No part of this publication may be reproduced in any form or by any means (including photocopying or storing it in any medium by electronic means and whether or not transiently or incidentally to some other use of this publication) without the written permission of the copyright owner, except in accordance with the provisions of the Copyright, Designs and Patents Act 1988 or under the terms of a licence issued by the Copyright Licensing Agency, 5th Floor, Shackleton House, Hay's Galleria, 4 Battle Bridge Lane, London, SE1 2HX (www.cla.co.uk). Applications for the copyright owner's written permission should be addressed to the publisher.

Printed and bound in Great Britain by Bell and Bain Ltd, Glasgow

Acknowledgements

The author and publisher would like to thank the following individuals and organisations for permission to reproduce photographs:

The publisher would like to thank the following for their kind permission to reproduce their photographs:

(Key: b-bottom; c-centre; l-left; r-right; t-top)

akg-images Ltd: 13; **Alamy Images:** Allstar Picture Library 23, 27r, CTK 16, dpa picture alliance 17, INTERFOTO 15b, ITAR-TASS Photo Agency 22, Keystone Pictures USA 10, MARKA 2, Pictorial Press Ltd 19r, Sputnik 19l, World History Archive 14; **Getty Images:** AFP 8, Gamma-Keystone 27l, Hulton Archive 15t, ool CHUTE DU MUR BERLIN 19, Popperfoto 9, Tony Duffy 25, ullstein bild 12; **Mary Evans Picture Library:** WEIMAR ARCHIVE 5

All other images © Pearson Education

Picture Research by: Alison Prior

Notes from the publisher
1. In order to ensure that this resource offers high-quality support for the associated Pearson qualification, it has been through a review process by the awarding body. This process confirms that this resource fully covers the teaching and learning content of the specification or part of a specification at which it is aimed. It also confirms that it demonstrates an appropriate balance between the development of subject skills, knowledge and understanding, in addition to preparation for assessment.

Endorsement does not cover any guidance on assessment activities or processes (e.g. practice questions or advice on how to answer assessment questions), included in the resource nor does it prescribe any particular approach to the teaching or delivery of a related course.

While the publishers have made every attempt to ensure that advice on the qualification and its assessment is accurate, the official specification and associated assessment guidance materials are the only authoritative source of information and should always be referred to for definitive guidance.

Pearson examiners have not contributed to any sections in this resource relevant to examination papers for which they have responsibility.

Examiners will not use endorsed resources as a source of material for any assessment set by Pearson.

Endorsement of a resource does not mean that the resource is required to achieve this Pearson qualification, nor does it mean that it is the only suitable material available to support the qualification, and any resource lists produced by the awarding body shall include this and other appropriate resources.

2. Pearson has robust editorial processes, including answer and fact checks, to ensure the accuracy of the content in this publication, and every effort is made to ensure this publication is free of errors. We are, however, only human, and occasionally errors do occur. Pearson is not liable for any misunderstandings that arise as a result of errors in this publication, but it is our priority to ensure that the content is accurate. If you spot an error, please do contact us at resourcescorrections@pearson.com so we can make sure it is corrected.